photoshop elements 4

Gone Wild

photoshop elements 4

Dave Huss

WILEY

Wiley Publishing, Inc.

Gone Wild

Photoshop® Elements 4 Gone Wild

Published by
Wiley Publishing, Inc.
111 River Street
Hoboken, N.J. 07030
www.wiley.com

ISBN 13: 978-0-7645-9991-0
ISBN 10: 0-7645-9991-7

Manufactured in the United States of America

10 9 8 7 6 5 4 3 2 1

1K/SU/QS/QW/IN

For general information on our other products and services or to obtain technical support, please contact our Customer Care Department within the U.S. at (800) 762-2974, outside the U.S. at (317) 572-3993 or fax (317) 572-4002.

Wiley also publishes its books in a variety of electronic formats. Some content that appears in print may not be available in electronic books.

Library of Congress Control Number: 2005931150

About the Author

Dave Huss has written more than 28 books on digital photo editing that have been translated into eight languages. A photographer for 40 years, his photo compositions and montages have won several international competitions. A popular conference speaker, he has taught classes and workshops on digital photo editing both in the US and Europe. Dave has also been seen on CNN and TechTV. A third-generation Texan, Dave lives in Austin, Texas.

Credits

Book Designer
LeAndra Hosier

Acquisitions Editor
Tom Heine

Project Editor
Timothy J. Borek

Technical Editor
David Herman

Copy Editor
Scott Tullis

Editorial Manager
Robyn Siesky

Vice President & Group Executive Publisher
Richard Swadley

Vice President & Publisher
Barry Pruett

Project Coordinator
Adrienne Martinez

Graphics and Production Specialists
Lauren Goddard
Jennifer Heleine
Lynsey Osborn
Ron Terry

Quality Control Technicians
Joe Niesen
Brian H. Walls

Proofreading and Indexing
Arielle Mennelle
Johnna VanHoose

Dedicated to David and Carol Bloom,
who have been and remain good friends
since our high-school days
so long ago.

Preface

This book is crazy. It goes beyond the pedestrian, mundane stuff that populates some of the other numerous titles staring back at you from the book shelves. This book assumes that you want to get a little wild with your digital photos. The pages of this book contain the kind of fun stuff I like to do with photos, like replacing the image of a president on a U.S. twenty-dollar bill with the face of my neighbor or engraving my favorite expression on a tombstone. (It was difficult to pick only one considering a host of ideas I get from the *Simpsons* Halloween specials.) Changing the reality in a photo is fun, but the ultimate goal of the tasks in this book is to not only create unique photo compositions but to make them look real; not real like the covers of supermarket tabloids with their photos of three-headed animals and extraterrestrials playing golf with the president; does anyone believe *those* are real? The true measure of success of the tasks in this book is for you to be able to create an image that causes a viewer to look several times and wonder if it is real. If you really do your job well, even after close scrutiny, the viewer walks away not absolutely convinced it is a fake.

If you think this photo trickery sounds like visual mischief, you're right, and I learned the art from the best. As a young man I apprenticed at Walt Disney Studios and was amazed to discover what these brilliant animators would draw when others weren't looking. My earliest memory of these visual high jinks was a beautifully drawn image of Mickey and Donald in a sleazy nightclub looking very drunk and smoking cigars. This penchant towards visual high jinks continues with me and others to this day. Many people who work with photos on a computer day in and day out have manipulated photos in ways that you don't want to know about. After a brief chuckle, most of this photo mischief ends up in the recycle bin, but even though it is trashed, every time you play with an image, you learn something new. I find those people that mess up photos the worst are usually the most creative at their craft.

As you go through this book you will discover some cool things that you can do with Adobe Photoshop Elements that may surprise you. After all, to do really great stuff you need Photoshop CS2, right? I too was once an unbeliever when it came to Elements. When I was teaching at Photoshop World many years ago, I was introduced to a man who was the product manager of Photoshop Elements (the original version), and the first words out of my mouth were, "So how badly did you have to cripple Photoshop to make Elements?" which, to his credit, he took surprisingly well. As it turned out, as I did more and more work with digital photography (and less with film photography), I discovered that rather than being a "crippled version," Elements was actually a version of Photoshop focused on the needs of the digital photographer. At the time Elements was introduced, Photoshop was more focused on the creation of Web pages. Even though the current version of Photoshop is now clearly targeted to the professional digital photographer, I still find it easier to perform my pixel magic using Elements than with CS2 — no kidding.

You probably want to ask two questions. The first question is: Who can use this book? A quick answer is, anyone with a basic knowledge of Photoshop Elements. That answer doesn't tell you much. To amplify my answer, here was the design goal of the book during creation. My project editor and I worked on the assumption that the reader already knew how to open and close files, right-click a mouse, and open and close palettes, so the tasks were constructed and laid out so that you, the reader, just needed to follow the directions. When possible, I included suggestions for varying the tasks so you can make different versions so all of the fun stuff you create doesn't always look the same. The bottom line: you don't need to be an artist, or a Photoshop Elements expert to use this book. The second question is: Must I have Photoshop Elements 4 to use the book? Not really, of all of the tasks in this book, there are only a few that use features only found in Photoshop Elements 4, and those are indicated in the task description before you begin. If you have yet to upgrade to Elements 4, you will be able to do almost all of the tasks in this book.

Here are some considerations about doing the tasks in this book. You will retain a lot more by downloading the sample images from www.wiley.com/go/elementsgonewild and actually doing the exercise. Most of the techniques described in the book take only a few minutes to create. In cases where a complicated selection is required, I have already made the selection for you and included it in the PSD file. My goal was always to keep the amount of time it takes you to do the task to a minimum. After all, you don't want to invest a lot of time in an image that you will never use — no one has that much time to waste.

So, there you have it. I hope you enjoy the tasks shown in the book and more importantly that you can come up with your own variations. In many cases, I think that you can build upon the tasks in this book and come up with results that are even wilder than the ones that I have created.

Acknowledgments

This is the part of the book that reads like a speech by an Oscar winner. Let's face it, when you see your favorite actor or actress at the awards ceremony grasping the golden statue their acceptance speech is usually a list of all of the people they want to thank before their time runs out. The differences between the Academy acceptance speech and this acknowledgement section are that this acknowledgment has no time limit and while the speech is watched by over a billion people around the world, this section will be read by at least a dozen, maybe more. Now that movie credits include everyone involved in a production (absolutely everyone), you have an idea of how many people it takes to create a movie. A book is also like a movie in that you don't see the host of skilled people that are needed to get a book from my computer to the shelf. This book you are holding represents the combined efforts of a large cast of hard-working craftspeople and artists. If I listed everyone who made a contribution to this edition, it would take up a large number of pages. So like a winning speech at the Academy Awards with a three-minute time limit, here are the people (coworkers and friends) that I want to recognize for their efforts.

First of all, I want to thank the crew on the Adobe Photoshop Elements development team who worked long and hard to create this version of Elements. Special thanks to Adobe's Mark Dahm, who patiently listened to my ranting and raving during the early stages of the product development.

I want to thank my acquisitions editor, Tom Heine, who had to constantly juggle the book schedule to keep up with my erratic contributions. Many thanks go to my hard-working project editor, Timothy Borek, who somehow was able to take hundreds of figures with questionable numbering and forge it into a book and was still able to find time to become a papa for the second time.

I especially want to thank all of the people that let me use their pictures in the book. I must also include thanks to my wife of 31 years, Elizabeth, who puts up with long absences while I had my face glued to a display while creating the tasks shown in this book. Well, my time is up, and my final thank you is to all of those who buy these books because without you, all of this effort would be for naught.

Contents

one **media exposure** 2

Magazine Cover Layout 4

At the Movies 9

Pulp Fiction 13

Pulp Fiction II 16

The Stamp Act 19

We're on the Money 24

Making It in Television 28

Making It on HDTV Television 33

15 Minutes of Infamy 35

two morphing and cloning around **38**

How Are You Fixed for Blades? 40

Family Resemblance 45

A Head for Figures 49

I Vant to Pump You Up 53

Morphing Steer Horns 56

three eye trickery **60**

Photos Cubed 62

Variations of Photos Cubed 67

Creating Cool Cones 69

I've Been Framed 73

Welcome to My World 77

Glass Spheres 80

Eyeball Highball 83

Making Pop-Up Pages 89

four wild photo effects 92

Give Me That Old-Time Photo 94

Late Night Church 99

Sports in Motion: Faking a Multiple Exposure 107

Flower Power 111

Alien Sky with Windmills 116

five making photos into paintings 122

Still-Life Masterpieces 124

Producing a True Watercolor Edge 128

People Painting 131

Master Image for Multiple Effects 133

Getting the Lead Out 137

A Different Approach to Making Watercolors 141

Airbrush Art 145

Colored Pencil Drawing 147

Faded Poster Print 150

six wild art effects 154

Change My World 156

Signs of the Times 160

Size Is Relative 165

Twisted Steel 169

Going Oriental 173

Heavy Metal Butterfly 176

seven special effects. 182

A Walk in the Clouds. 184

Isolated Color 187

Patriotic Eagle 190

New Paint Job for Cars 193

A Monumental Task. 196

Producing Puzzling Effects 202

eight wild text effects. 206

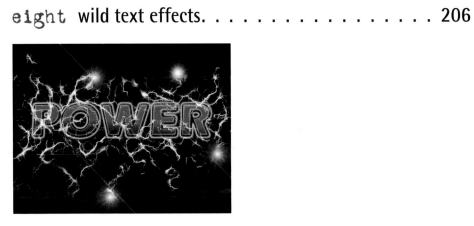

The Power of Gold 208

Opposites Attract 211

Old and Dirty Type 215

Awesome Power Type 219

Stone Cold Text 223

Weathered Copper Text 226

Twisted Text 229

Rock Star Text 231

media exposure

In the future everyone will be famous for fifteen minutes.

–Andy Warhol, (1928 - 1987)

Fame isn't all it's cracked up to be. Even Andy Warhol got sick of it. "I'm bored with that line. I never use it anymore. My new line is, 'In fifteen minutes everybody will be famous.'" Ironically, no one remembers or quotes the "new line." Because we are such a media-saturated culture I felt it apropos to begin this book with a chapter about the many ways you can use Photoshop Elements to make yourself or someone you know famous, even if it is only on your computer. Most of the techniques in this chapter are not only easy, but they are fun to do, so let your imagination run wild.

Magazine Cover Layout

In this task, you learn how to make and place someone on a magazine cover. The candidates for such a treatment are too numerous to list, but here are a few: Making a cover with a parent as *Time* magazine's Man or Woman of the Year, putting your beloved pooch on the cover of *Horse and Hound* (which would be even more meaningful to you if you saw the movie *Notting Hill*), or placing a photo of your favorite Little Leaguer on the cover of *Sports Illustrated* are just a few examples of what you can do with this technique.

1. Open the image polkadot model.psd. Using the Magic Wand tool (W) with Contiguous selected in the Options bar, select the background. You will need to Shift+select to include the two major areas of the background.

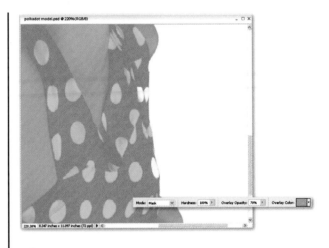

3. Now we need to put the model in front of a blurred background. Select the Move tool (V), change the zoom to Fit on Screen (Ctrl+0) and invert the selection (Ctrl+Shift+I). Open background.psd and, using the Move tool, drag the model into the background. Close polkadot model.psd and don't save the changes.

2. Some of the white dots on the woman's dress got included in the background selection. Zoom in on them and use the Selection Brush tool with the Mode set to Mask to remove them from the background selection. Because the default mask color and her dress are red, you may want to change the color and increase the opacity of the mask so you can see what you are doing.

TIP

You can correct mistakes made with the Selection Brush by painting back over the area while holding down the Alt key.

4 A small amount of the white background was captured with the model. Photoshop Elements 4 has a greatly improved Defringe feature, so choose Layer, Defringe and pick a value of 3 pixels to remove the white fringe.

5 To add the title of the magazine, change the foreground color to white, select the Horizontal Type tool, and in the Tool Options bar change the Font to Impact and the size to 115 points. Because the font is so large, if you leave kerning on Auto, the space between the lines will be too small; so change the Kerning in the Tool Options bar to a value between 100 and 103. Click inside the image and type in **SPOTS ILLUSTRATED**. Select the Move tool and position the text near the top, then choose the Low Drop Shadow from the Drop Shadows library in the Styles and Effects palette. The font selection and its position is designed to simulate a nationally known sports magazine. Using their real name in this example could result in a popular sporting event called Parachuting Lawyers. For suggestions on making your personal magazine covers look like the real deal, see the sidebar *Making Your Cover Look Real*.

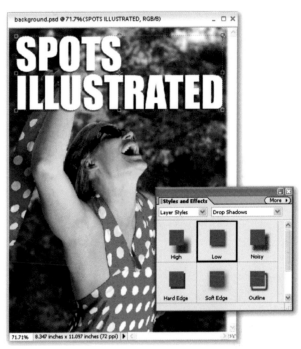

6 This magazine uses one or two rectangle shapes that serve as a background to text describing a lead story inside the issue. Using the Eyedropper tool (I), select the red of the model's dress as the foreground color by clicking on it. Choose the Rectangle Shape tool (U) and drag a shape as shown. To ensure the shapes are the same height, right-click on the shape in the Layers palette, choose Duplicate Layer, and then use the Move tool to align them as shown.

7 Right-click on the shape layers in the Layers palette and choose Rasterize Layer before adding the Low Drop Shadow from the Styles and Effects palette. Change the foreground color to white before selecting the Text tool to add the text to each one. Change the Font to Aril Black at a size of 18 and the Leading in the Tool Options bar back to Auto before adding your text.

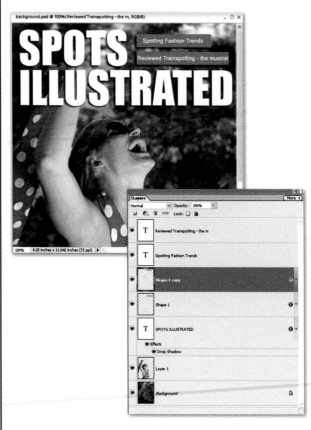

⑧ All magazine covers have a box somewhere on the cover for the date and other such stuff. This particular magazine uses a black box with the date and its Web site. Use the Shape tool and Type tool to add that as shown, and then use the Type tool to add the title of the cover story.

Making Your Covers Look Real

Making a fake magazine cover look real is relatively easy. Every established magazine has its trademark appearance. The faux (sounds cooler than fake) cover we just created was *Sports Illustrated*, a magazine that always uses a photo that covers the page and a heavy sans serif font in all caps for its title. Youth culture magazines are fond of bright florescent letters with a distressed grunge look in the background. The key to a successful faux cover is to capture enough of the visual clues that are consistent with the magazine you want to represent, and the reader's mind will usually fill in any missing parts. Some magazines, like *Wired*, use its logo for the title. This is a little more work, but a logo can be captured from an issue of the magazine using a scanner. Lastly, I must add a warning: Making fake covers of respected national publications is fun, but be careful what you do with the photos. If you want to sell these creations, you may discover the owners of larger magazines keep a ready supply of lawyers who have had their sense of humor surgically removed. First amendment issues sound great on TV shows, but real defense attorneys cost money. Have fun, but respect copyrights.

9 The cover (as shown) is complete, but there is one important variation that needs to be considered. For the past few years, most magazines have been placing the photo of the subject over part of the magazine title. So as a variation, you can drag the title layer in the Layers palette so it is below the layer containing the model.

At the Movies

With the dazzling effects of The *Lord of the Rings, Star Wars,* and *Harry Potter* films, one thing is perfectly clear: People enjoy fantasy. When it comes to creating visual representations of these unreal figments of our imagination, we assume that it is something that can be done only with a multimillion-dollar effects studio. The truth of the matter is, it is not that hard to create some pretty wild effects using just your digital camera and Photoshop Elements (PSE). In this technique we will take a photo of a pretty wild custom-made vehicle and convert it into a science fiction scene for a standard of the movie business: the movie still.

1 Open the image monster car.psd. The first step is to select the monster car to isolate it from the background. You might be thinking that with a complex subject like the mechanical monster, it would take some time to create an accurate selection, and you would be right. It took me about 40 minutes. For those that don't want to spend the time creating a complex selection (I know I wouldn't) I have included the selection in the image file. Choose Select, Load Selection, and then choose background, making sure to check the Invert check box. Click OK and that's it.

TIP

Everyone has his or her favorite way to create a selection. Mine is to make a rough selection around the subject with the Lasso tool, and then fine-tune the selection with the Selection Brush, not forgetting to include the background peeking through the parts of the machine and the driver. It's usually best to use a Magic Wand tool in Subtractive mode to remove these areas.

2 Copy the contents of the selection to the Windows clipboard (Ctrl+C) and close the image. Next, open the image fire.psd and paste the contents of the clipboard onto it (Ctrl+V) as shown.

3 At this point all of the flames are behind the subject, so we need to make the flames appear as part of the background, not on top of it. To achieve this effect we need a layer mask, something very familiar to Photoshop users, but you will not find anything labeled Layer Mask in Photoshop Elements. We'll need to use a workaround that acts just like a layer mask. Choose Layers, New Adjustment Layer, Levels. You could label the Adjustment Layer with the name Layer Mask, but it isn't necessary. Click OK, and then OK again. Nothing appears to have happened at this point.

4 Right-click on the background and choose Duplicate Layer. Then, click OK to close the Duplicate layer dialog box. In the Layers Palette, drag the duplicate of the fiery background to the top. Now the monster has disappeared. With the top layer selected, apply Group with Previous (Ctrl+G). At this point you still cannot see the monster. Now comes the cool part. Select the Layer Mask Thumbnail on the Adjustment layer in the Layers Palette. Choose the Brush tool in the Toolbox, and with Black as the foreground color begin painting on the image (not the thumbnail) where the monster should be. *Voilà*, it begins to appear. Everywhere you paint black on the top "layer mask" becomes invisible. So you can selectively paint away the top layer of flames to make flames appear to be surrounding the metal monster of mayhem as shown.

5 The monster is made of shiny metal, and it seems logical that the orange color of the flames would be reflected in the metal. Select the Eyedropper tool (I). In the Tool Options bar, choose a 5x5 sample size and then click somewhere in the orange flames. The foreground color is now a flame orange. Select the layer containing the monster, and then choose the Brush tool with a low opacity (20%) and the Blend mode set to Linear Burn. Begin painting all of the bright metal parts, and don't forget the driver: he may not be metal, but he reflects the light produced by the flames as well.

6 Zoom in on the area of the eyes before changing the color of the brush to red and making the blend mode Color Burn. Make the brush smaller and change the black eyes of the monster into red ones. Next, change the brush to white with Normal blending mode and put a glint on the eyes as shown.

7 Change the brush color to blue and the blend mode to Overlay to make the driver's glasses bright blue. While you have the brush handy, you may consider putting tiny colored dots on the joints (mine are blue), coloring some of the hoses, and adding color to the panels.

8 For a finishing touch, we need to do something — anything — with the white plastic speaker. There is just something about a cheap white plastic speaker that takes away from the whole I'm-going-to-conquer-your-puny-little-planet look we are trying to achieve. Rather than clone it out, let's make it into the power source for the machine. Let's face it: With the price of gas the way it is, he's going to need a power orb to get around. The best part is that the effect is easy to create. First, create a circle selection on top of the speaker. Use the Clone Stamp tool (S) to fill the selection with flames.

9 Change the foreground color to white and, with the Brush tool set at a normal blend with an opacity of 15%, highlight the upper inside edges. Use a combination of Dodge and Burn tools to make the flames inside the orb stand out. Invert the selection (Ctrl+Shift+I) and use a dark color to darken the speaker (aka power orb energy coupling). Over that paint a light overcoat of orange, which is the color reflected by the orb.

10 To give it a space fantasy touch, deselect (Ctrl+D) the selection we created, select the background in the Layers palette, and apply a lens flare on the background behind the orb using the Movie Prime setting. Select the top background copy and apply the same filter again (Ctrl+F). The completed image is shown next.

11 To make it look like the movie stills that are passed out with Hollywood press kits, use the Canvas tool (Image ⇨ Resize ⇨ Canvas Size) to add a one-inch white border around the image. Next, apply Canvas size again, except add one inch to the bottom. Use the Type tool to add the text. To make it look like the real thing, put lots of line credits.

I demonstrated several techniques in this task. Remember that you can use these blending techniques just as well when making a photo montage of your family — even if they don't contain metal monsters or flames.

The Return of the Metal Munching Moon Mice
This time it's mechanical

A Toxic Wasteland Production - Directed by Steven Oilspillburg, Produced by Exxon Valdez, Screenplay by Fo Maldahide,
Based on a true story that never happened. Starring Mel Glibsome, Russel Cro, Holly Bury, and introducing Egor the Wonder Moose.
Copyright 2012

Pulp Fiction

Most photos can be made to have a comic book appearance. The task is relatively simple, but there is one issue that you should be aware of before you begin. One of the obvious visual clues that an image is a comic is the halftone pattern, the use of which made the artist Lichtenstein a rich man. The problem with this halftone pattern occurs when it is viewed at less than 100%, when the image is resized. In either situation the halftone pattern causes a moiré to develop, which appears as a weird checkerboard pattern. So, if the image will be displayed on the Web, make it smaller than you normally would; and if the image is going to be printed, ensure that it is the correct size so that some well-meaning graphics person doesn't have to resize it.

1. Open the image sad woman.psd. In the Layers Palette, make two duplicate layers of the background as shown.

2. Select the middle layer in the Layers Palette. Choose the Minimum filter (Filter, Other, Minimum) and use a setting of 3 pixels. Unless you turn off the upper layer you will not see the immediate effect of this filter.

3 Next, apply the Poster Edges filter using Edge Thickness set to 1, Edge Intensity set to 1, and Posterization set to 3.

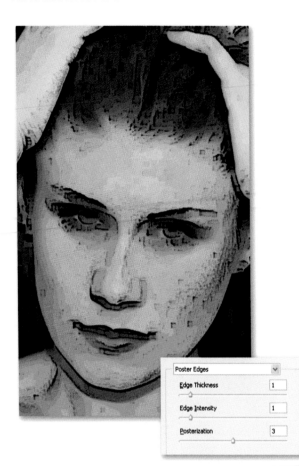

TIP

If Tool Tips are enabled in Preferences (Edit, Preferences, General), the name of the shape appears when you position the cursor over it.

5 Now, it wouldn't be a comic without the balloon. In this case, the woman appears to be thinking, so we need a thought balloon. Before beginning, make sure the foreground color is white (unless you like black thought balloons). Add a new layer on top of the image, and with the layer selected, choose the Custom Shape tool in the Toolbox. From the Tool Options Bar choose the thought balloon called Thought 2. Click on the image and drag out the desired shape. You may have noticed that it is facing the wring direction. You can easily flip it by using the Move tool (V), grabbing the middle control handle and pulling it across itself, which causes the shape to reverse. Double-click on the balloon when you have it positioned and shaped the way you want.

4 Select the top layer and apply the Color Halftone filter (Filter, Pixelate, Color Halftone) using the settings shown. After applying the Color Halftone, change the blending mode of the layer to Overlay.

6 Select the Type tool, change the foreground color to white, and change the Font to Comic Sans MS (what else could you use?). Enter the thoughts that she is thinking. Be careful what you put here: she's my daughter. Because Photoshop Elements 4 now supports paragraph text, you can type as many lines as you want. To keep the lines of type close together, you have to change the Leading from Auto to a number that is just a little larger than the type size you are using. After you have entered the text and positioned it in the thought balloon, you are almost finished making a comic panel.

7 The last things to clean up are the dark pixilated areas that were produced by applying Minimum filter back in Step 2. In the Layers palette, we need to turn off all of the layers except the one above the background. The quickest way to do that is to hold down the Alt key and click on the eye icon for that layer. This makes all of the other layers invisible. This is a good trick to know if you work with layers a lot. With the other layers turned off, you can see the dark areas on the image and use a Stamp Clone brush to remove them.

8 Alt-click the layer icon and the finished image appears. In case you were wondering what purpose the background layer serves, it is there as an untouched copy of the original; so at any time or at any client whim you have access to the original within the file instead of floating around somewhere on your hard drive. Having the original in the file isn't necessary, but it is a good habit to get into.

Pulp Fiction II

Although movies may have caused a resurgence of comic book heroes, it was the pop-art culture and Lichtenstein who made these masterpieces of halftones into art. If you want your 15 minutes of fame to be recognized in the pop-art culture, here is another technique that can quickly turn a photo of someone you know into a masterpiece.

1 Open trumpet player.psd. If you look at the Layers palette you will see it contains two layers. Select the middle layer and apply the Watercolor filter (Filter, Artistic, Watercolor) using a Brush Detail setting of 13, Shadow Intensity of 0, and Texture of 1. Because the top layer prevents you from seeing the middle layer, you will not see any change.

2 Select the top layer and apply Glowing Edges (Filter, Stylize, Glowing Edges) using and Edge Width of 2, Edge Brightness of 10, and a Smoothness setting of 6.

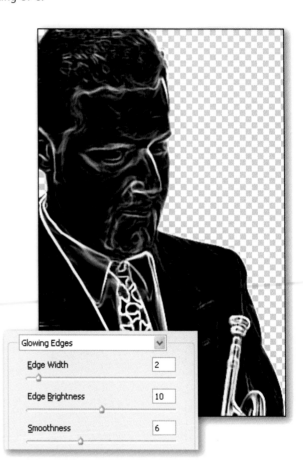

3 Open the Hue/Saturation dialog box (Ctrl+U) and reduce the Saturation to -100.

4 Invert the colors in the layer (Ctrl+I) and apply the Crosshatch filter (Filter, Brush Strokes, Crosshatch) with a Stroke Length of 6, Sharpness of 9, and Strength of 1.

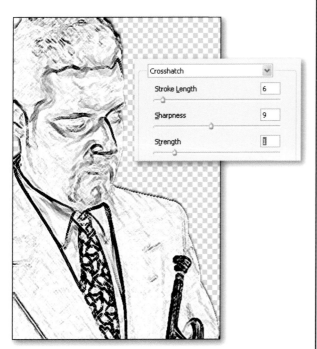

5 Change the blending mode of the top layer to Overlay. Because this is pop art, we need to make the colors a little more saturated. Select the middle layer, open Hue/Saturation, and increase the saturation to +30. To complete the trumpet player component of this project, select the top two layers and merge them together.

6 The next part of this masterpiece involves making a suitable background for the musician. Create a new image that is 800 x 600 pixels and use the Paint Bucket Tool to fill it with yellow. For best halftone results, use the settings shown in the Color Picker dialog box. Apply the Color Halftone filter (Filter, Pixelate, Halftone) at a setting of 8 pixels.

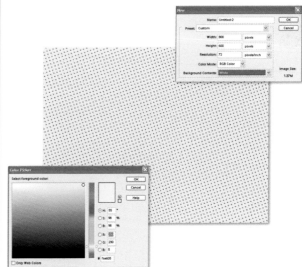

7 Open the trumpet player image, and from the Layers palette select the combined layers and drag them into the yellow background image. Use the Move tool to position him in the upper left corner.

8 Use the Rectangle tool (U) and drag two shapes to form the borders of the comic art as shown.

9 Because in this image we want the subject to be talking, select the Custom Shape tool, select Talk 1 from the drop-down list in the Tool Options bar, and drag

a balloon shape on the image. To give it the classic Lichtenstein look, apply a Low Drop Shadow style to the talk balloon as shown.

10 All that needs to be done is to add the text that the subject will be speaking. In case you were wondering, what the trumpet player is saying is a great quote from the movie *Playing by Heart*. For a finishing touch, add the copyright information. I wonder if there really is a Moose Breath Comics out there somewhere.

This next song is called Talking about Love is like Dancing About Architecture

© 2005 Moose Breath Comics

The Stamp Act

If you are not into comics and consider pop art to be too lowbrow, another public forum on which we see the faces of famous people is the postage stamp. In the real world, getting your mug on a stamp takes a long time, second only to the time necessary to becoming a saint. So, why should we have to wait for the postal service to get around to putting our favorite people on a stamp? Using Photoshop Elements you can convert a photograph into a single postage stamp and combine those into a sheet of stamps. The procedure for converting a photo into a postage stamp isn't hard, but it does involve making several parts. Having said that, let's begin.

1 The first step is to create the base image and set up the rulers and grid settings. Create a new 500-x-500-pixel image at a resolution of 100 dpi. From the View menu, turn on the grid and rulers. Double-click one of the rulers on the image to open the Preferences and change the Units to Pixels. Select Grid settings from the Preference drop-down list and change the settings as shown. Change to the default colors (D).

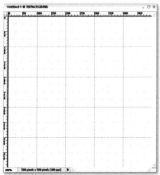

2 Now we need to set up the brush. Select the Brush tool and change the size to 50 pixels (px). Open More Options and change the settings as shown. To accurately view the grid, you need to be viewing at 100% (Actual Pixels). Add a new layer on top of the background (Shift+Ctrl+N).

3 Locate the first point, which is 50 pixels to the right and 50 pixels down. The brush shape should fit within the grid square. With the top layer selected, click the brush one time, making a black circle as shown. Holding down the Shift key, click on the second point on the grid and the Brush tool makes a series of circles between the two points. Continue to do this until the image looks like the one shown.

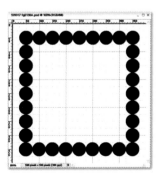

4 Select the Paint Bucket tool. With the Tolerance set to 50, click on the area inside the circles and outside of the image, completely filling the outer area with black.

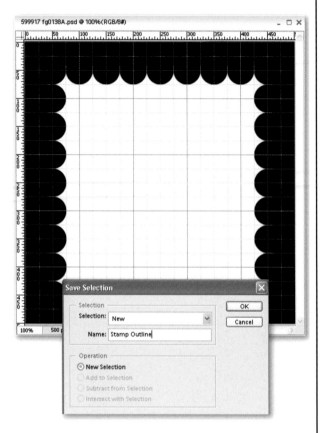

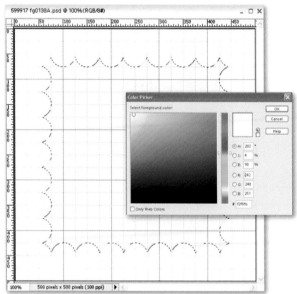

6 Convert the scalloped stamp background we just created into a layer (Shift+Ctrl+J). From the Styles and Effects palette, apply the Soft Edge Drop Shadow and you have a perforated stamp foundation. I recommend that you save it for use the next time you want to make your own postage stamps.

5 Use the Magic Wand tool to select the white area and save the selection as Stamp Outline. Although you will not need the selection later in this task, you should get into the habit of saving selections with the image. Delete the layer, change the Background color to a very pale blue as shown, and click inside the selection.

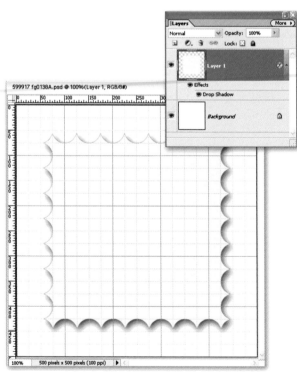

In this example, I made the perforations quite large, but you can change the size of the perforations by reducing the initial brush size.

7 To give the photo the appearance that it actually belongs on the stamp, you need to first create a pattern. Create a new file that is 10 x 10 pixels at 72 dpi with a transparent background. Zoom in to 1600%. Use the Pencil tool and make a two-pixel-thick line as shown. Make it into a pattern (Edit, Define Pattern) named Horizontal 1. Close and don't save the pattern file.

8 Open the image man with glasses.psd. With the top layer selected, choose Edit, Fill Layer, and select Pattern from the Contents drop-down list, choosing the pattern you just named. Check the Colorize option in the Hue/Saturation dialog (Ctrl+U) and use the settings as shown. Only the photo of the man changes. You can pick any Hue setting that you want; I was going for the fake duotone look that is so popular on stamps and currency. When you are finished, flatten the image (Layer, Flatten Image) and resize it to 300 x 300 pixels. Resizing the image softens the overall appearance without losing the edges.

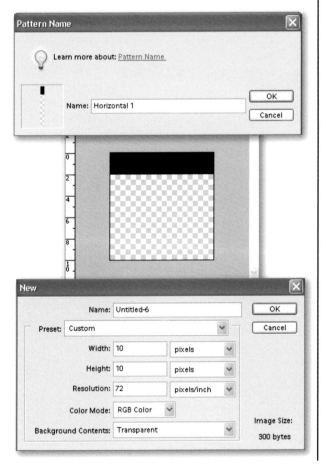

9 Select the entire image (Ctrl+A) and copy it (Ctrl+C) to the Clipboard. Select the scalloped stamp image and paste it (Ctrl+V) as shown. Close the image of the man with glasses without saving any changes.

10 Add the text. You can use any font; the font used in the example was Copperplate Gothic Bold. When the text is in place, apply the Drop Shadow Style Low.

11 There is one last step that, although unnecessary, I think adds a touch of greater realism. Select the scalloped edge layer and lock the transparency at the top of the Layers palette. Apply a small amount of Uniform Noise as shown.

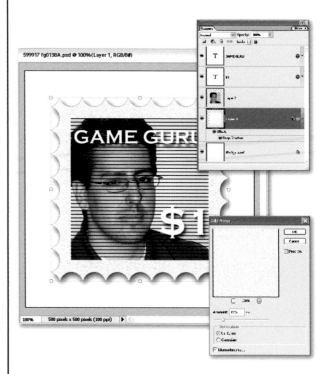

12 Where do we go from here? There are several possible variations. First, because the scalloped edges and the photo are on different layers, you can use the Hue/Saturation command (Ctrl+U) to change the hue and saturation independent of one another. Because we typically see stamps sold in sheets, use the Canvas Size to make the background larger and duplicate the stamp you made enough times to make a sheet. After you have a sheet there is still a lot more you can do. By merging together the layers containing the stamps, you can use the Transformation tool to apply some Perspective and the Liquify Filter to even put a small curl on one of the stamps. For the ultimate touch of realism, remove one or more of the stamps; using the Transformation tool, you can even have one of the stamps dangling by its perforation, as shown here.

We're on the Money

Getting your face on a U.S. postage stamp is difficult enough in real life, but nothing when compared to what it takes to get your mug on U.S. paper currency (see the sidebar "Whose Face is on U.S. Paper Money?"). Ironically, with Photoshop Elements it is much easier to get your face onto U.S. currency than it is to make a postage stamp.

Because there hasn't been a woman on U.S. paper currency in over a hundred years, it is time we corrected that injustice. She needs to be highly influential, a national leader, so the choice is obvious — Oprah.

Many in this country no longer have a clue as to who those people on bills are (exceptions being Washington and Lincoln), so it's time to replace them with influential people that everyone knows and respects — that would be The Simpsons. Because the $100 bill is the largest note in general circulation, it seems only right to put Montgomery Burn's image on it.

To accomplish this task, we need a photograph of some currency. You cannot scan the currency because Photoshop Elements has a filter to prevent that. The laws regarding photographing U.S. currency have relaxed over the past ten years, but although you cannot go into the business of making your own money, you can have some fun photographing and playing with the images.

1. Open smiling face.psd, which is the head of my neighbor floating on a layer. I thought he made a good choice. He looks presidential and his eyes are closed — perfect. After selecting the top layer, the first step is to change his colors to match the currency. If you were thinking green, you are only partly right. The color of greenbacks these days is more of a gray with a slight green tint. Open Hue/Saturation (Ctrl+U) and change the settings as shown.

(2) Add a new layer (Shift+Ctrl+N) and choose Fill layer from the Edit menu. Apply the pattern Horizontal 1 that was created in Task 5. You now have lines running through the image as shown. Apply the Wave filter (Filter, Distort, Wave) to the layer containing the pattern, using the settings shown. This creates wavy lines that look like an engravers work, and it also creates a slight optical illusion. Did it appear that the face got distorted when you applied the Wave filter? It didn't, but it does look like it did. To make the lines appear only on the face, change the Blending mode for the pattern layer to Color Burn, and then duplicate that layer again so there are two pattern layers.

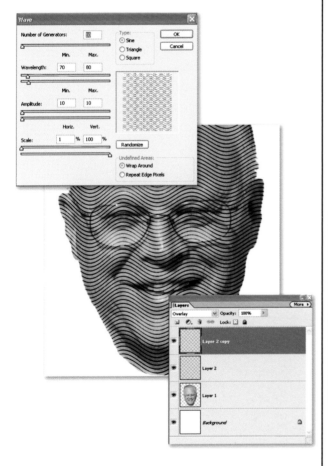

(3) Merge the layers. Load the selection (Select, Load Selection...) named Outline. Copy (Ctrl+C) the head into the Clipboard and close the file. Don't save any changes. Open money.psd and paste (Ctrl+V) the head as a new layer. The head is very large in comparison to the background, so use Transform (Ctrl+T) to resize the head and rotate it slightly so it looks like the one shown. In this case, the portrait of Franklin is taken at a different angle than the shot we are using, making Franklin's head appear wider. Use the Transform to make the new head roughly the same shape as the one being covered up.

TIP

Try to do all of your transformations before clicking the Commit button or double-clicking. If you commit your transformation every time you make a change, the image becomes soft and mushy. Don't worry about the appearance when you are reshaping the head, as Photoshop Elements displays a crude approximation of the image until the change is finally applied. The following screen shots show what the image looks like while the transformations are being performed and how the image appears when the transformations are finally applied.

TIP

When working on images that have fine lines, it is best to view them at 100% (Actual Pixels).

4 To fine-tune the image, you first need to get rid of the white fringe that is apparent around the edges. Choose Enhance, Adjust Color, Defringe Layer.... From the dialog box apply a value of 3 pixels. This tool was greatly improved in Photoshop Elements 4 and should remove most of the white fringe. Next, use Hue/Saturation to make the colors look more like the background, then use the Eraser tool set to a low Opacity to remove parts of the new face that don't belong. Also use the Clone Stamp tool to move parts of the original background to fill in spots where the face doesn't quite line up with the original.

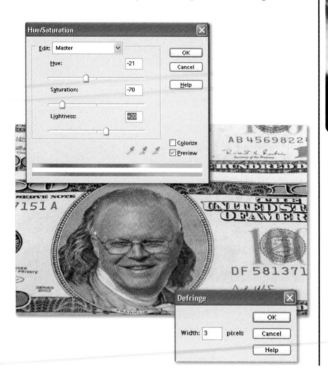

Whose Face is on US Paper Money?

It is a commonly held belief that you must have once been a president to have your face on U.S. paper money. Although most of the faces adorning the U.S. bills were once presidents, there are several exceptions. The examples we see most often are Alexander Hamilton ($10), Benjamin Franklin ($100), and the one seen least often is Salmon P. Chase ($10,000). The former and latter were both Secretary of the Treasury, and good old Ben was included because he and his printing press set up the paper currency system we use today. The president on the Trillion Dollar bill is Harry S. Truman, but you would have to be a diehard *Simpsons* fan to know that. You might be interested to know the only woman to ever appear on a U.S. note was Martha Washington. Her portrait appeared on the face of the $1 Silver Certificate of 1886.

5 The last part is relatively simple. When you have the replacement head exactly the way you want it, make three copies of the layer, resize them, and replace the faces on the other bills. The topmost bill is out of focus, caused by Depth of Field limitations. That is the one image that you may need to slightly blur to make consistent with the rest of the bank note at the top of the image.

Making It in Television

Ever since television made its appearance back in 1949, people have wanted to be on it. It is somewhat ironic that in our security-conscious environment, most people are actually on TV much more than they realize. Whether it's on a local station or a national program, to be on TV counts toward the fabled 15 minutes of fame. In this task, I show you how to bring your favorite photo into both an old black-and-white TV and a modern TV. I begin by making someone look like they are on an old-style TV circa the 1950s. So, let's set the Wayback Machine to November 1955 and change a photo into a 50s TV program using a photo of Bob, my barber for the past 28 years.

1 After opening the photo of Bob.psd, your first step is to crop it so it fits the 4:3 aspect ratio. Select the Crop tool (C), change the dimensions in the Tool Options Bar to Width 4 and Height 3, and crop the image as shown.

2 Change the color to grayscale (Image, Mode, Grayscale) and add a new layer (Shift+Ctrl+N).

Making Your TV Mockups Look Authentic

To make an old-style black-and-white TV show appear convincing, you should consider a few guidelines. First is the aspect ratio of the screen (the ratio of height to width). Before the days of widescreen all TV screens had a standard aspect ratio of 4:3, so you should crop the image to that ratio right from the start. Second, the images they produced were low contrast and noisy (grainy) which makes transforming images so they look like old black-and-white TV images is a great way to showcase poor-quality photos. A very telling visual clue for both the old and the new TV images is the presence of scan lines. These scan lines are produced by the picture tube in the TV as it paints the image on the inside of the screen. All of these are suggestions to make an image look like it really might have been on TV.

③ If you didn't make the pattern Horizontal 1 in Task 6, create a new file that is 10 x 10 pixels at 72 dpi with a transparent background. Zoom in to 1600%. Use the Pencil tool and make a 2-pixel-thick line as shown. Make it into a pattern (Edit, Define Pattern) named TV SCAN 1. Close the pattern image you just made and don't save it when asked.

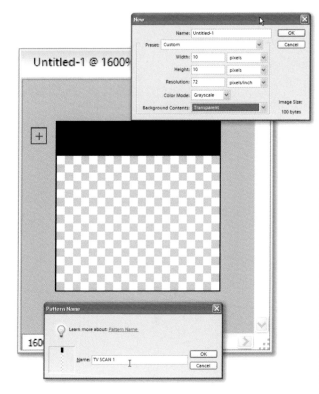

④ Choose Fill Layer from the Edit menu, choose Use Pattern in the Contents section, and select the TV SCAN 1 made in Step 3 to create the appearance of scan lines running through the image as shown. The resulting scan lines may appear a little harsh, but that is why we put them on their own layer: so that their appearance could be adjusted. For the moment, turn off the scan lines you just created by clicking the eye icon in the Layers palette.

⑤ At this point you could put the image into a photo of an old TV chassis and call it quits, but there are a few more touches to make it look real enough for a magazine cover. The first problem is that the quality of the photo is too good, so select the background and open Brightness/Contrast (Enhance, Adjust lighting, Brightness/Contrast) and use settings similar to those shown. The goal is to lighten the image while reducing the overall contrast. The actual settings used on other photos is dependent on the contrast of the image you are working on.

TIP

Be aware that viewing the scan lines at any zoom level other than 100% (Actual Pixels) produces moiré patterns that make some of the lines appear distorted or missing. This phenomena affects only viewing and has no effect on the actual scan lines.

6 Back in the early days of television the station ID often was displayed in the lower corner of the screen. Create a new layer above the background but under the scan lines, and use the Horizontal Type tool to create a station ID. Because graphic generators back then were pretty primitive, use a simple typeface. I used Gill Sans MT Condensed at a size of 14 points. In the same way, create the title of the show. For this I chose the Impact typeface at 30 points.

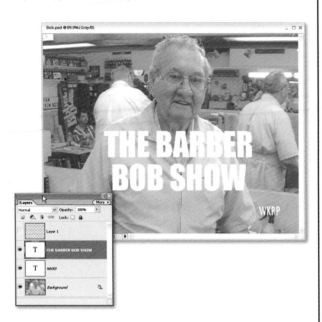

7 The text looks sharp and crisp, which is not right for this medium. In the Layers palette Shift+select both type layers. Right-click on the layers and choose Rasterize Type. Right-click again and choose Merge Layers. Finally, apply a Gaussian blur at a setting of 1 pixel.

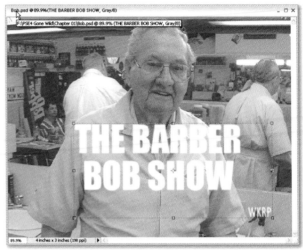

8 Make the layer containing the scan lines visible again and apply the Gaussian blur settings to it (Ctrl+F). Change the Opacity setting for the layer to 50%.

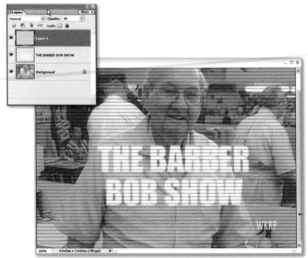

15 Minutes of Infamy

I am not sure if Andy Warhol considered having your photo on a wanted poster was part of his 15 minutes of fame, but it is a good way to complete this chapter. Because making a realistic, current wanted poster might not be very funny to some people, I show you a quick way to create an old-time wanted poster.

1 Open smiling man.psd and select the top layer. Choose the Graphic Pen filter and change the settings to those shown in the figure.

2 Open the file old paper.psd, and click and drag the image from the smiling man image on top of the old paper. The smiling man image will appear as a layer in the Layers Palette of the old-paper image. Change the Blending Mode at the top of the Layers Palette to Overlay.

3 Add the text for the poster and use the Color Blend mode on its type layer. This will appear too light, so duplicate the layer and place the duplicate layer on top of the first to make it even darker.

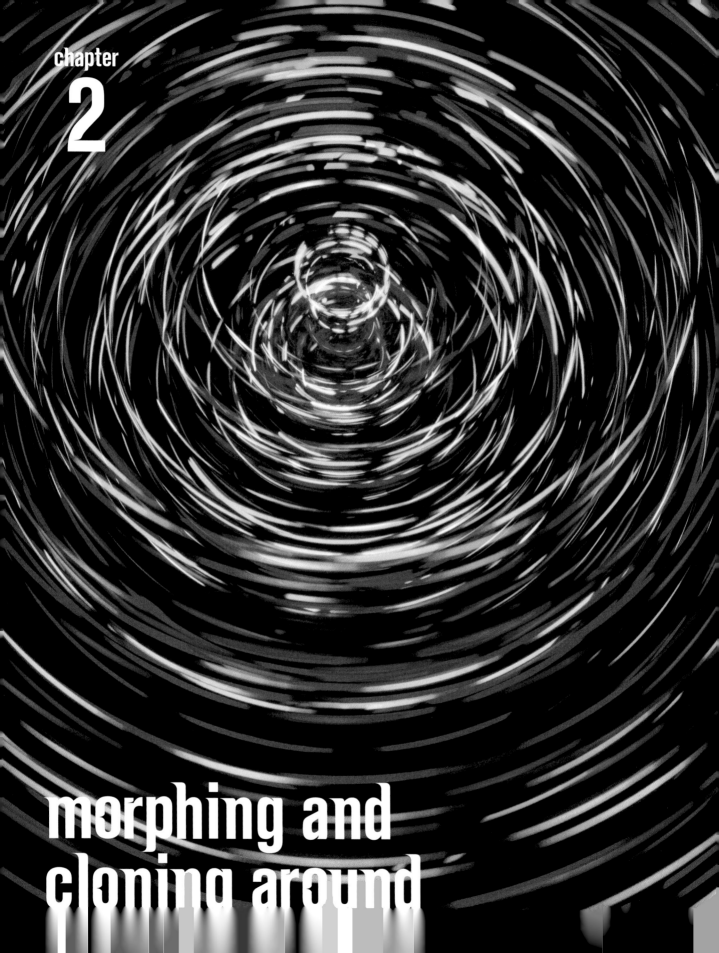

chapter

2

morphing and cloning around

The camera never lies. This was an adage that was popular when I was growing up, the idea being that a photograph could only be an accurate representation of the subject. Back in the late 1950s, our lives contained several fundamental truths: The government did not lie and the camera could not lie. Between Watergate and digital photography, both of these mantras have changed. This chapter covers several tasks that can change the reality originally captured so radically as to make any camera output not only lie but appear positively pathological.

How Are You Fixed for Blades?

There seems to be some competition between razor manufacturers over how many blades are needed to produce a satisfactory shave. Using a picture of a multiblade razor as a starting point, in this task you make your own major improvement to the science of shaving. The Clone Stamp tool and a few other tricks can help you change this mild-mannered razor into the ultimate mega-turbo razor.

1 Open the image razor.psd from the book's Web site. Using the Polygonal Lasso tool, select the area of the razor head as shown.

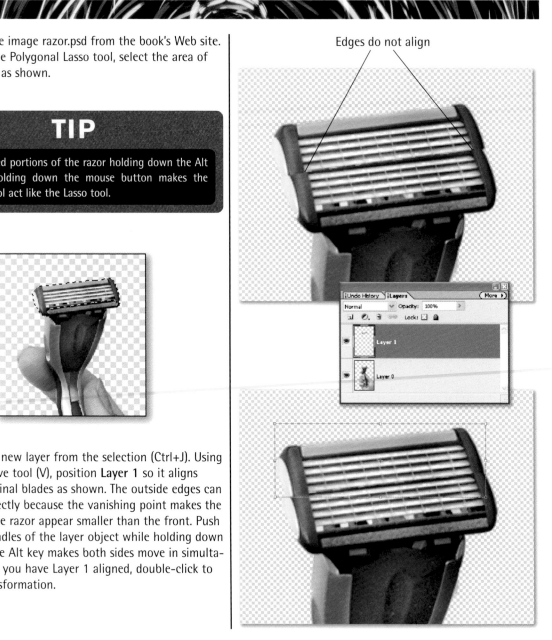

Edges do not align

TIP

For the curved portions of the razor holding down the Alt key while holding down the mouse button makes the Polygonal tool act like the Lasso tool.

2 Make a new layer from the selection (Ctrl+J). Using the Move tool (V), position **Layer 1** so it aligns above the original blades as shown. The outside edges can not align perfectly because the vanishing point makes the back end of the razor appear smaller than the front. Push in the side handles of the layer object while holding down the Alt key; the Alt key makes both sides move in simultaneously. When you have Layer 1 aligned, double-click to apply the transformation.

3 Duplicate Layer 1 by dragging it onto the Create a New Layer icon in the Layers palette. Repeat Step 2 to make the new **Layer 1 Copy** fit the razor. Don't worry about the edges; you'll fix that later. After both of the two new layers are aligned, merge the top two layers.

Create a new layer

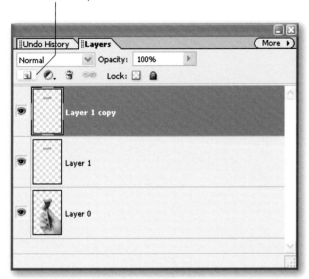

4 When all of the layers are aligned, merge everything into a single layer. At this point, the razor looks more like a flyswatter, so you need to make the blades wider. Create a selection like the one shown. The edges of the selection are not critical since the area around the razor is transparent. Convert the selection into a layer (Ctrl+J). Holding down the Alt key, drag the layer handles out until the new blades look like the one shown. Double-click the Layer 1 to apply the transformation.

5 Use the Polygonal Lasso tool to create a straight edge along both the edges as shown. I changed to a blue mask color so you can see the selection better. Use the Eyedropper tool and select a lighter gray that matches the rest of the razor and paint along the right edge.

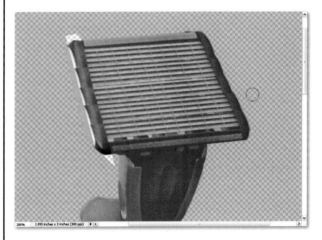

6 Next, use the Eyedropper to select a darker gray and paint the left side. The finished edge of the razor is shown.

7 To smooth the light blue plastic backing, you need to have a background to be able to see the new edge you are going to create. Add a new layer by clicking the Create a New Layer icon in the Layers palette. Apply a fill layer (Edit ▷ Fill Layer) at 50% gray and drag it under the razor.

8 You can see how uneven the blue plastic is. As in Step 5, use the Polygonal Lasso tool to create a straight line along the edge of the blue plastic. Use the Eyedropper tool to select a color that matches the blue and recreate the edge.

9 The perspective of the razor still isn't right, so select the top layer and use Transformation (Image ▷ Transform ▷ Distort) to correct the perspective of the razor.

10 Double-click to apply the transformation. Merge the razor and head into a single layer.

11 Razors should be wet, so here is how that is accomplished: On the razor.psd image, add a new layer on top and change its blending mode to Darken. Open Water.psd from www.wiley.com/go/elements-gonewild; this file serves as a source for the water drops.

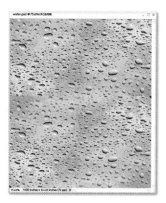

12 Select the Clone Stamp tool and using Water.psd as a source. Place the tool back on the Razor image and use the Stamp Clone tool to paint drops on the razor as shown.

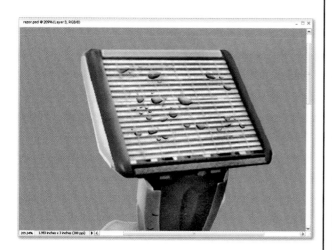

13 The gray background of water.psd may dull the background of the razor on which you applied the water drops. When this happens, use the Dodge and Burn tools to remove the unwanted background, setting the Dodge tool for Highlights (40% Exposure) and the Burn tool for Shadows (40% Exposure). Applying these tools removes any unwanted backgrounds but leaves the water drops.

14 Replace the background by opening the file Green tile.psd, and dragging the tile image on top of the razor image. It becomes a layer in the Layers palette. Drag the green tile layer to the Background.

Using this same technique, I added some text and put water drops on both the text and the background.

Family Resemblance

A popular late-night talk show likes to combine the characteristics of different celebraties to see what their children might look like. Although it would be great to have our own fun with some celebrities, just the thought of doing so causes several of the lawyers for this fine publication to have sleepless nights. The many ways you can combine people could fill up the rest of the chapter. In this task, I show you the basics.

1 Open the photos Tim.tif and Grace.psd.

2 Drag the photo of Grace onto Tim. Her image becomes a layer in the Tim image. Close Grace.

③ Change the opacity of the layer to 50%, making it semitransparent. Use the Transformation command to resize the top image. The size of the image in this task makes resizing necessary. You can resize it from the corner but the mouth of the top image will not overlap the bottom one. Click the bottom handle and push it up until the images match as shown. Change the layer opacity back to 100% and double-click to apply the transformation.

④ Create a fake layer mask (because Elements doesn't have one). In the Layers palette, select the Background. Add a Levels adjustment layer (Layer➪New Adjustment Layer➪Levels) Click OK both times the OK button appears. Select the top layer and group it (Ctrl+G) with the adjustment layer. Select the Adjustment Layer Mask thumbnail and fill it with black (Edit➪Fill Layer). The layer disappears.

TIP

To get the best effect, you should try to make both subjects roughly the same size. The need for same size is especially important when aligning major facial features.

9 To give him a background, open olympic stadium.jpg. This is a photo taken in Athens of the stadium that was built in 1896 and serves as a perfect backdrop.

10 Drag the man action figure we just created onto the stadium photo. Create a new layer on top of the Background by clicking the Create a new layer icon in the Layers palette. This will be **Layer 4**.

Working with Linked Layers

You can link layers together, so all of the linked layers can be moved as a single unit, helping you manage layers. Select a layer from the Layers palette. You can link layers together in the Layers palette by selecting the layers and then clicking the Link Layers icon. To unlink the layers, click on the Link Layers icon again or right-click the selected and linked layers and choose Unlink Layers. Because multiple layers in an image increase the file size, you can reduce the file size by merging layers when you are done editing.

11 Select the Brush tool and paint a soft shadow under the character. Add some text, and you have completed the project. To preserve the position of the objects on different layers, you can Link the layers together. If this was a project for a customer you should keep the resulting image as a PSD file (preserving the layers). For the image that you want to share with others, you should Flatten the image (Layer➪Flatten Image).

I Vant to Pump You Up

Bodybuilding has become extremely popular in the past 20 years. Everyone seems to want flat six-pack stomachs and bulging biceps. Getting the pulsating pectorals usually requires many hours at the gym, and some people even take steriods. Using the Liquify command in Photoshop Elements provides a quick and fun way to add muscle to your photos. Changing a body shape with this tool is called *body sculpting* by some; I just call it fun. Before we begin, just remember a little truth about changing someone's body shape: What is funny (read hysterical) to you can and may hurt other people's feelings, which can make them feel so bad that they hire an attorney to help you feel their pain. Just be considerate when radically changing someone else's shape. Now let's make some muscle!

1 Open the file strongman.psd and choose the Liquify command (Filter⇨Distort⇨Liquify). The Liquify dialog box appears, covering the entire screen. The major tools on the left, from top to bottom are Warp, Turbulence, Twirl Clockwise, Twirl Counter Clockwise, Pucker, and Bloat.

2 Change the Brush size to one big enough to encompass the arms that we want to enlarge. In this example, I set the brush size to about 180 pixels. Select the Bloat tool and, placing the brush over his left forearm, click and hold as the arm area under the brush gets larger.

TIP

The Liquify dialog box may or may not fill the entire screen. You can adjust its size like that of any other window by simply dragging any edge or corner.

3 Next, move the brush to the upper arm and expand the arm as shown.

Preventing Popeye Syndrome

The one major challenge is making the new expanded arms appear to be like real muscle and not Popeye. To achieve this requires an understanding of what body builders look like. Look at magazines or images on web sites to get a visual understanding of what you want. The primary tool that should be used is the Bloat tool in the Liquify dialog box. Although it is tempting to make the tool diameter very large, a large brush has a tendency to also make adjacent body parts grow as well. You will have better results using a small tool diameter to isolate the growth of the tool to a small area of the body part. The other important ingredient is patience. Be prepared to experiment and use Undo (Ctrl+Z) when strokes don't work as expected.

4 Repeat Steps 2 and 3 on the man's right arm.

5 Apply the Warp tool (W) to the bottom of the image and push in on either side of his waist. This makes his chest region appear more built up.

6 Behold the completed bodybuilder. You know what they say: No pain . . . no pain!

Morphing Steer Horns

Morphing transforms a shape image or object smoothly from an initial state to a different final state. Some graphics professionals refer to the process as *tweening* (from the presence of in-between states). Even though the definition sounds really dull, morphing is anything but dull. Morphing is a way to combine two completely different objects and make them into a seamless new creation. You will not find a Morp tool anywhere in Photoshop Elements, but in this task you discover how to transform, or morph, the tip one of the horns of a longhorn steer into a banana.

① Open the photo longhorn.psd. The first step is to remove the tip of the horn. Since you do not need the original horn tip again, in the next step we will use the Clone Stamp (S) tool to replace the horn with grass background.

③ Open the file banana.psd and, using the Move tool (V), drag the banana from its image onto the longhorn photo. Then, close the image banana.psd without saving any changes.

② Select the Clone Stamp tool, and in the Options bar uncheck the Aligned checkbox. Hold down the Alt key and click a point on the grass background near the horn tip to serve as a source point for the Clone Stamp tool. Paint the horn tip with the Clone Stamp tool until the grass has replaced the entire horn as shown.

TIP

Because the Aligned option is unchecked, each time you release the mouse button the Stamp Clone tool resets the source point to its original starting point.

4 With the banana selected, press Ctrl+T to allow transformation of the banana to resize (scale) it so the thickness of the banana is roughly the same thickness as the horn.

5 The key to making the smoothest possible transition between the two dissimilar objects is to use a clipping mask. Officially, Elements doesn't have a clipping mask, but making one is easy. In the Layers palette, select the Background and create an Adjustment Layer (Layer ⇨ New Adjustment Layer ⇨ Levels). When asked, name the layer **clipping mask** and then click OK without making any changes to the Levels settings. Select Layer 1 (the one containing the banana) and group it with the clipping mask (Ctrl+G).

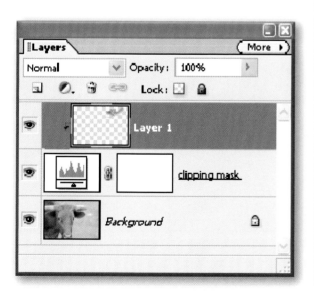

6 To use the clipping mask, select the thumbnail mask of the clipping mask layer. Change the foreground/background colors to their default (D). Select the Brush tool (B) and paint the portions of the banana that you want to be transparent. Although it seems you are actually painting the banana, you are actually painting the clipping mask. All pixels in the mask that are painted black appear transparent; if they are painted white, they become opaque. Paint the left side of the banana until it blends into the horn as shown.

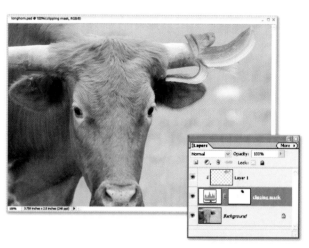

TIP

Press the X key on the keyboard to quickly switch between foreground and background.

7 Once you have the banana blended with the horn, use Transformation (Ctrl+T) to drag the right edge to stretch the banana out towards the edge as shown and you're finished.

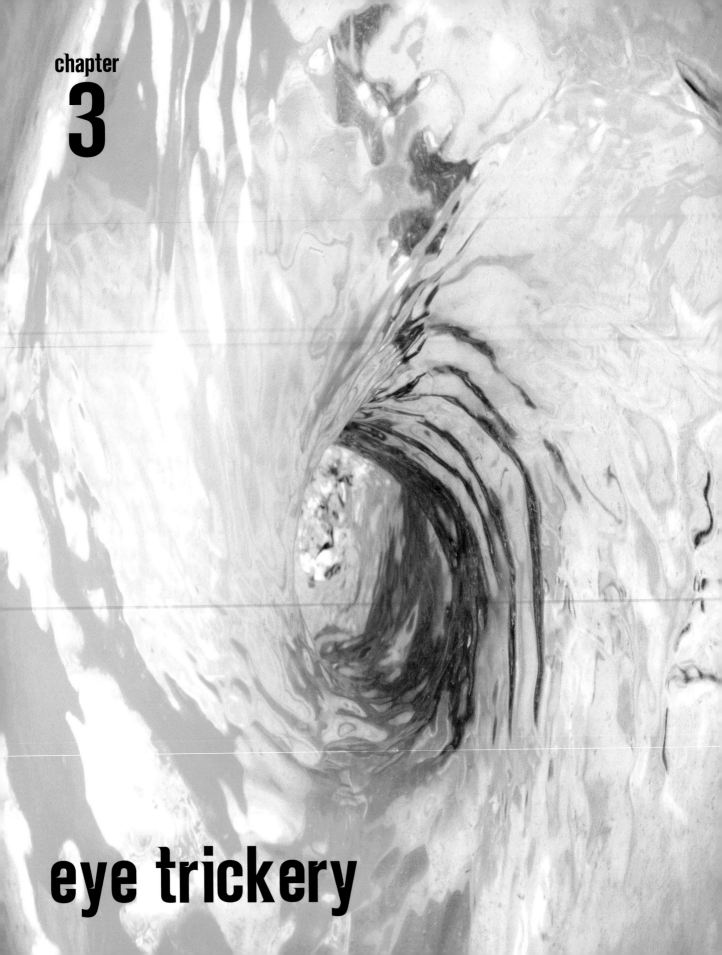

eye trickery

Trompe l'oeil is the name given to the style of painting which achieves a three-dimensional appearance. In other words, the painted object is suppose to trick the viewer into believing the object is actually real. From the French word trompe l'oeil, pronounced "trum ploy" this French word literally means "trick of the eye." In the first two chapters, we created 2-D effects that produced a little eye trickery. In this section, we explore how to make these objects appear 3-D without wearing the funny glasses.

Photos Cubed

Even though Photoshop Elements is not a 3-D program, you can make very convincing 3-D shapes out of almost any photo or parts of a picture. This task creates a simple photo cube and uses the grid, transformation tools, and a little bit of shading to achieve the 3-D effect.

1 Create a new 800-x-600-pixel image that has 24-bit color with a white background. Change the grid preferences to Color: any color works OK, Style: Lines, Gridline every 100 pixels, Subdivisions: 4. Turn on Snap to Grid in the View menu.

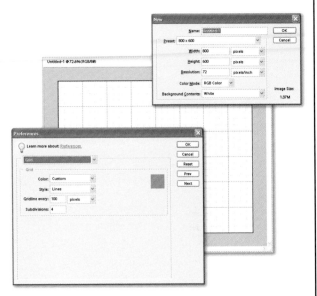

2 Open Child.psd and with the Move tool click+drag the photo onto the new image. Close Child.psd.

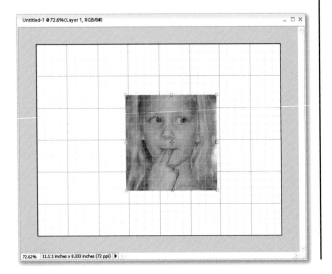

3 Duplicate the layer containing the child image and make it invisible by clicking the eye icon in the Layers palette. Select the Skew transformation tool and drag the right control handle up to the next major gridline (400 pixels). Double-click the image when the transform is done to apply the transformation.

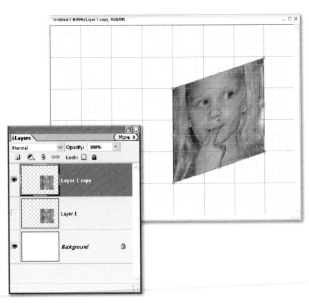

chapter 3 • eye trickery

④ Duplicate the layer you just transformed. Flip the layer (Image➪Rotate➪Flip Layer Horizontal) before dragging it over to align with the bottom layer.

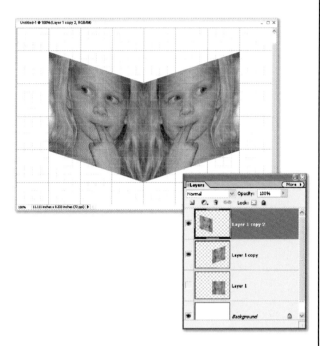

⑥ In the Layers palette, Shift-select the two visible layers, right-click on them, and then choose Link Layers. In the image window, drag the linked layers to the bottom of the image window so they barely touch the bottom edge.

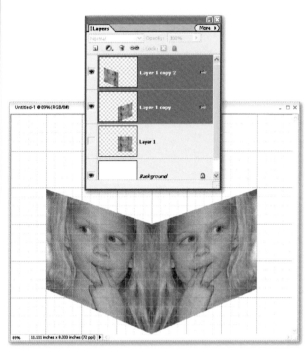

⑤ At this point, the cube doesn't look right to the eye because the sides do not exhibit the slight perspective the mind expects. Select the Distort transform tool (not Perspective). Click on one of the layers and click+drag the lower outside control handle up one grid (100 pixels). When finished, double-click the layer to apply the transformation before selecting the other layer and repeating the same procedure.

Click here

Drag edge up 100 pixels

(7) Make the invisible layer visible and drag it to the top position in the Layers palette. Select Distortion Transformation (Ctrl+T) and drag the two lower handles of the layer as shown before dragging the other two handles to their respective positions. When completed, double-click the layer to apply the transformation. Link all three layers together and move the cube back to the center of the image window.

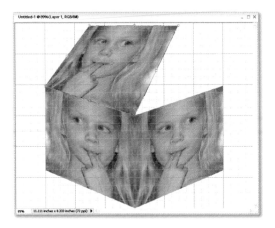

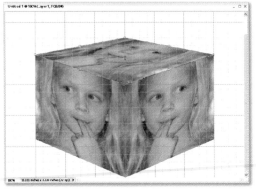

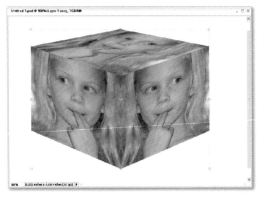

(8) To achieve the appearance of depth we need to add some shading. Decide from what direction your light source is coming to determine where to add appropriate shading. Assuming the light is coming from the upper right of the image window, the side facing away from the source would be in the shadows. Rather than darken the entire side using Levels, use the visual trick that produces a stronger effect: Lock the transparency of the right side. Select the Brush tool at a low opacity (less than 20%), and drag the brush so that it overlaps enough of the layer edge to create subtle shading on the edges of the right side.

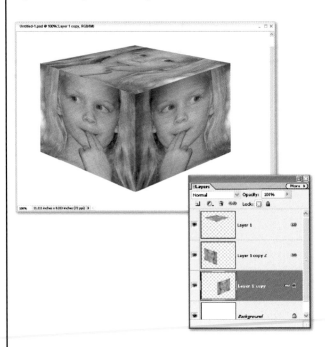

(9) Repeat the same technique to lighten the edges closer to the light source. Now that we have a cube floating on a white background, let's add some reflection. Select the left-facing side, duplicate the layer, and flip the layer vertically.

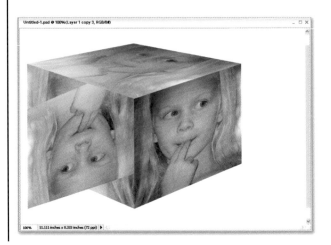

10 To accomplish this step, you must zoom out so you can use the handles that appear outside the image borders. Select the Skew Transformation tool and drag the left side of the reflection until the bottom of the facing side and the top of the reflection meet. Double-click the reflection to apply the transformation. Duplicate the reflection, flip the layer horizontally, and drag it over under the right-facing side.

11 Merge the two reflections together, and in the Layers palette, drag them so they are below the layers that make up the cube. Change their Opacity to 50%. Select the background and, using Styles and Effects, apply a Wood-Rosewood layer above the background.

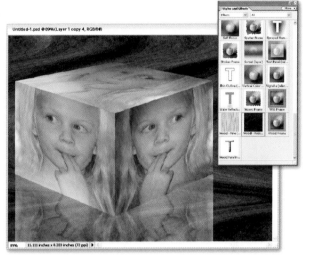

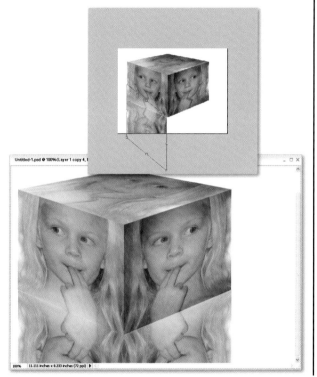

12 To make the wood layer look like the edge of a table, select the rosewood layer and drag a rectangle similar to the one shown. Move the middle slider of the Levels command (Ctrl+L) to the right until the background is very dark with little detail showing. Invert the selection (Ctrl+Shift+I) and use the Brush tool with white at a very low opacity to define the edge of the wood. The edges of the reflection are too sharp, so in the Layers palette select the reflection layer. Using the Eraser tool, paint over the edges with a soft, low-opacity brush stroke to reduce the sharpness of the edges. Finally, select the rosewood layer and, using the Brush tool at low opacity, paint a soft dark area on the wood to represent a faint shadow.

If you have the time, use a Brush tool with black at a very low opacity setting (12–18%) and dim some of the star groupings. To add a real touch of class, put a little color on the brush and paint in a few smudges of color.

Glass Spheres

Glass is a fascinating medium for the artist and the viewer. Its fluidity of shape, its transparency, and the endless types and patterns of distortortion produced when viewing objects through it makes it unique as it is beautiful. Creating the effects of glass is one of the few subjects that I can say is easier in Photoshop than in Photoshop Elements. That is because the layer styles in Photoshop have a vast number of adjustments available for the creation of very complex glass effects. Still, there is a lot you can do in Photoshop Elements, so let's get started. We begin with the simplest glass illusion of all — a flower in glass.

1 Open the image Blue Checkered Curtain.psd. Open the image Rose.psd and use the Move tool to click+drag the rose to the new image file as a layer.

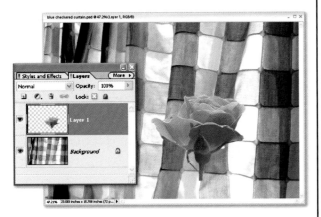

2 To create the outside diameter of the glass sphere we must first select the Elliptical Marquee tool. While holding down the Alt and Shift keys, drag the selection outward from the rose's center until the selection encompasses the entire rose. After making the selection, use the Elliptical Marquee tool to center the selection on the rose. Save the selection, (Select⇨Save Selection) because you'll need it later.

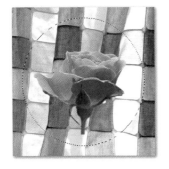

3 Select the background, make a new layer via copy (Ctrl+J), and then merge the rose with the new layer just created. The only change you see is in the Layers palette.

4 With the merged layer still selected, choose the Inner Glow layer style called Simple. Double-click to apply. A thin white line now surrounds the rose.

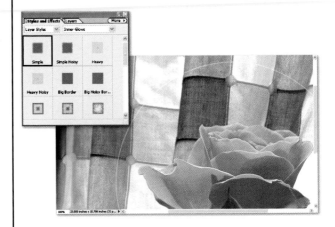

⑤ In the Layers Palette, double-click the Layers icon and change the Inner Glow size to 180 pixels. The circle surrounding the flower now has a soft diffused edge.

⑥ Lock the layer in the Layers palette and apply the Spherize filter (Filter➪Distort➪Spherize) at a setting of 60%.

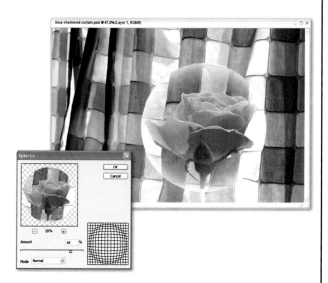

⑦ Add a new layer on top of the rose. Load the selection that was saved in Step 2 and, using the Brush tool, begin increasing the opacity of the white on the edges of the image as shown. Apply shading at a low

opacity, and then place a small glint of light before applying a Gaussian Blur to the entire top layer at a mild radius setting of 6 pixels. Deselect the image (Ctrl+D).

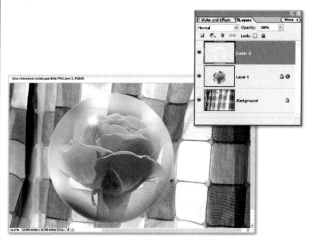

⑧ Now, make a stand to hold the ball. Click the Rounded Rectangular tool and drag a black shape below the glass ball. Simplify the shape by clicking the Simplify button in the options bar and then lock the layer in the Layers palette.

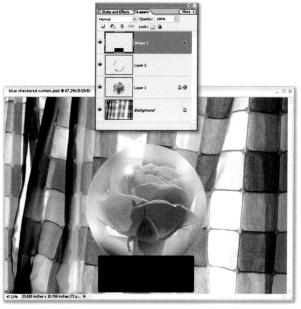

9 Select the Brush tool with Opacity set to 35% and create reflections on the black stand by dragging white lines on the shape. Holding down the Shift key while making the lines produces vertical lines. Next, use the Shape tool to drag a narrow horizontal shape across the base of the first shape. In the options bar, select the Black Glass style from the Glass Button category.

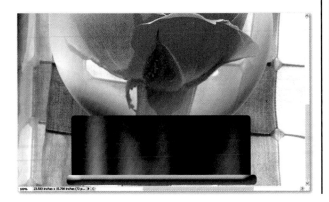

10 Simplify the layer and merge the two shapes together. Use the Perspective Transformation tool and drag the top of the shape so it fits the glass as shown.

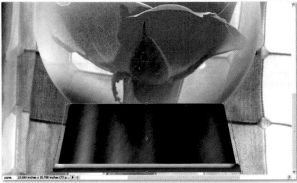

You have completed the image.

Eyeball Highball

Making a realistic eyeball is a challenge involving several hours of work. Making a reasonably realistic eyeball is much easier. Although real eyeballs are not perfectly symmetyrical, the one we are going to make doesn't have to pass a medical exam. To complete the task, we are going to float the eyeball by changing an empty glass into one that is either half empty or half full, depending on your point of view.

1 Create a new 400-x-400-pixel file that has a white background. Turn on the Grid and Snap to Grid in the View menu. Select the Elliptical Marquee tool and, while holding down the Alt and Shift keys, drag a circle from the center until you have a selection that is within one grid square of the edge. Make a layer of the selection (Ctrl+J) and lock the layer.

2 Use the Color Picker to change the background color to a light blue. Select the Gradient tool. In the options bar, choose a Radial Gradient using Foreground to Background. Click the Edit key and modify the gradient so it looks like the one shown. Beginning in the center of the circle, click and drag the Gradient tool out to the edge.

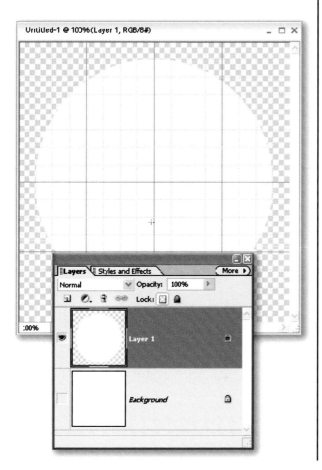

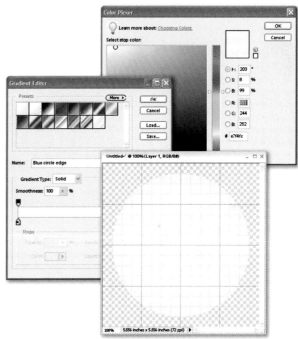

3 Add a new layer on top and drag a new circle selection from the center as shown. Change the foreground and background colors to black and your favorite eye color. I'm from Texas, so our eye color is brown. Enough said. Make a similar gradient with the Gradient editor, and use the Gradient tool to drag a line from the center to the edge of the selection.

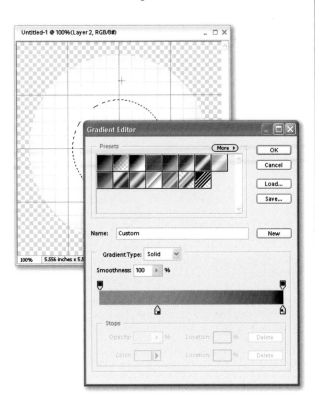

4 Apply noise to the center gradient that you just created with a setting of 40%, Distribution: Uniform, Monochromatic checked. Remove the selection and apply the Radial Blur filter (Filter⇨Blur⇨Radial Blur) at an Amount of 50, Blur Method: Zoom, and Quality setting of Good.

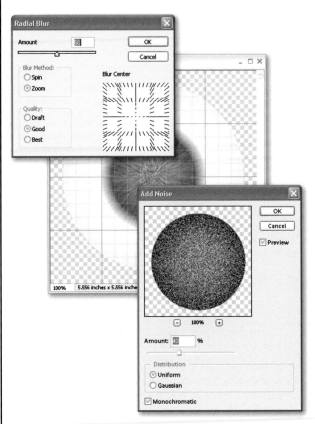

5 Select the Elliptical Shape tool and from the center hold down the Alt and Shift keys and make the pupil of the eye. The size of the pupil is a matter of personal preference. I tried to choose a size that was an average size. When the pupil is the size that you like, click the

Simplify button in the Options bar. Just for an extra touch of realism, apply some noise with the following settings: Amount: 20%, Distribution: Gaussian, Monochromatic: Checked. When everything is done, merge all of the layers together.

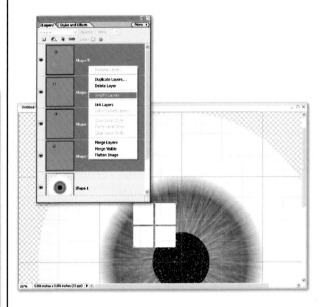

6 Eyeballs are wet and slimy, so we need to add a classic window reflection to give that appearance. Add a new layer and select the Rectangle shape tool, making the color white. Click and drag four identical squares next to one another on the grid on the top layer that was just created.

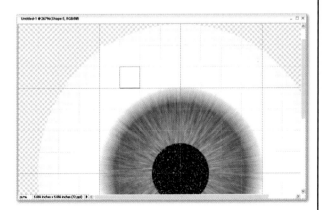

7 This is the tricky part. In the Layers palette, Ctrl-click to select all four layers (each shape is on its own layer), and then right-click and choose Simplify Layers. Select the top layer in the palette and use arrow keys on the keyboard to nudge the square away from the other shapes by two clicks. The goal is to end up with four squares that look like the one shown. When you have them aligned, merge them together. In the screen I have moved them in front of the iris so you can see them better.

8 Turn off Snap to Grid. Drag the shape over the edge of the eye and rotate it as shown using Free Transform (Ctrl+T).

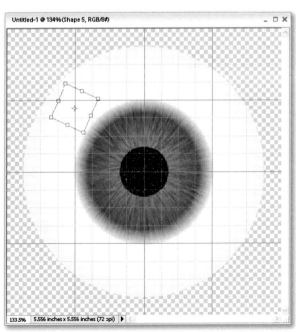

9 Apply the Spherize filter at 100%, Mode: Normal. This adds a curve to the traditional window reflection you just made.

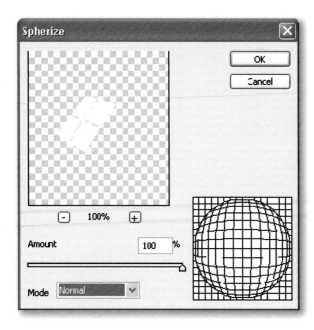

10 To finish the window reflection, use the Brush tool at a very low opacity (10%) to add some shadows near the edge. Also, use a hard brush to add a white glint near the pupil. When finished, you should turn off the grid and Snap to Grid and save the file as eyeball.psd, but keep the file open.

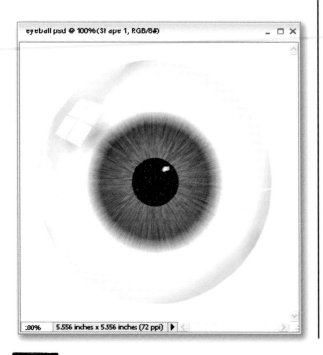

11 Now that the eyeball is finished, open Empty glass.jpg. Select the Elliptical Marquee tool and drag an ellipse like the one shown.

12 Use the Eyedropper to select a dark shade of brown reflected on bottom of the glass, making that shade the foreground color. Click the Paint Bucket tool inside the selection and then change the blending mode of the layer in the Layers palette to Hard Light.

$\overset{\text{\small 13}}{\textcircled{}}$ Invert the selection (Ctrl+Shift+I) and select the Brush tool. At 100% Opacity, paint the rest of the glass to make it appear full. Delete the selection.

$\overset{\text{\small 14}}{\textcircled{}}$ From the eyeball image, click and drag the eyeball into the glass. Close the eyeball file. Resize the eyeball using Free Transform (Ctrl+T).

$\overset{\text{\small 15}}{\textcircled{}}$ Create a new layer above the eyeball, and use the Brush tool at a low opacity (25%) to paint the part of the eyeball that would be submerged (do eyeballs float?) with the dark brown.

$\overset{\text{\small 16}}{\textcircled{}}$ Next, select the eyeball layer and lock the transparency. Change the foreground/background colors to their default (D), and at a very low opacity, paint some slight shading on the eyeball.

17 All you have left is to add the text. In this case, a quote by Rick from the movie *Casablanca* seems most appropriate.

Making Pop-Up Pages

There is just something cool about a pop-up in a book. I liked them as a kid, and now that I am older, much older, I still think the concept of a 3-D image popping out of a 2-D book is a lot of fun and it usually catches the viewer's attention. Unlike the last task, this is an easy one. The secret to making it work is to use a very low Zoom setting with some of the images so that they fill only part of the image window. So let's blast off with a shuttle launch. If you want to make more space-oriented images, NASA makes lots of their photos available to the public. Do a Google search for NASA images and you will be presented with a cornucopia of photos of every aspect of space travel.

(1) Open Shuttle launch.psd. Select the Magic Extractor (Image⇨Magic Extractor), which is new in Elements 4. In the dialog box that takes over the entire screen, select samples of the foreground and background using the respective brushes. Use the Preview function to determine if all of the background has been extracted. Once the background has been removed the next step is to use another photo for the background.

(2) Open Launch pad.psd and use the thumbwheel of the mouse to zoom back so it occupies only a small portion of the image window.

3 Use the Canvas Size command to change the size of the image to Width: 6 inches, Height: 2 inches, Relative checkbox checked, ensure the center anchor is selected by clicking on the center, Canvas extension color: White.

4 Use the Magic Wand to select the white portion of the background. Invert the selection (Ctrl+Shift+I) and make a new layer from the selection (Ctrl+J).

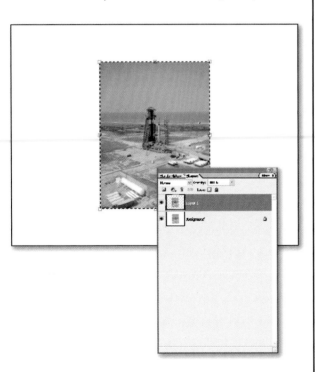

5 Select the layer in the Layers palette. Choose the Move tool (V) Select Free Transform (Ctrl+T). Right-click on the image and select Distort from the pop-up menu. Reshape the layer so it looks like the one shown. You need not be exact: even though the task contains rockets, it isn't rocket science. Use the grid to help you visually if you need to. When you have the layer as flat as possible, double-click on it to apply the transformation.

6 Returning to the Shuttle launch you worked on earlier in the project, click and drag the layer over to the launch pad image. Close Shuttle launch.psd without saving the changes. Use the Transformation Skew tool and drag down the right handle to align the bottom of the launch with the roads on the launch pad.

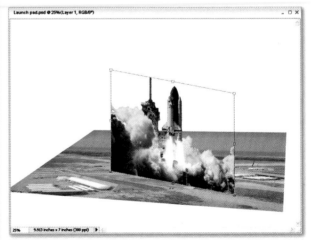

7 With the shuttle selected, use the Eraser tool to remove the square edges from the smoke clouds and you're finished.

wild photo effects

This chapter covers a broad range of wild photo effects, from making a photo taken with a digital camera look like it was photographed 100 years ago, to making an abandoned church appear to be having a late night meeting. This chapter is all about bending and twisting reality in digital images so much that even the supermarket tabloids would be jealous. You can use the techniques shown in this chapter in a wide variety of different applications and settings.

Give Me That Old-Time Photo

Ask advanced Photoshop Elements users how to age a photograph and they will tell you to add a sepia tint to it. Sepia toning is a photographic process invented over 100 years ago for the practical purpose of prolonging the life of a silver-gelatin photograph. Look through the old photos in an antique store and you will see more prints that are sepia toned than those that are black and white. But changing the color of the photo to sepia is just the first step in making your photo look like it has been around for 100 years.

1. Open Old building.psd from the book Web site, www.wiley.com/go/elementsgonewild. Open Hue/Saturation (Ctrl+U) and check the Colorize check box.

Drag the Hue slider to 38, the Saturation slider to 25, and the Lightness slider to +17.

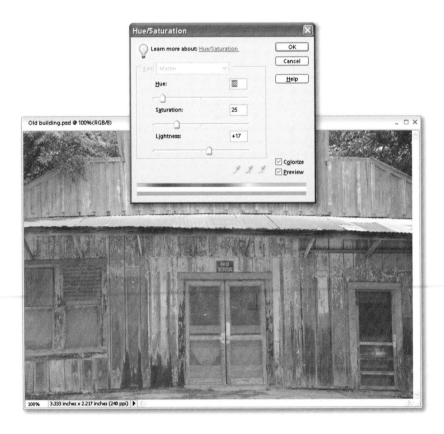

(2) Old photos have an uneven blotchy look caused by normal aging and the photo not being protected from the effects of sun over the years. Change the foreground and background colors to their Default (D) setting. To achieve this effect, you need to create several layers that produce an uneven distressed look. Add a new layer over the Background and fill the layer with Clouds (Filter⊏>Render⊏>Clouds).

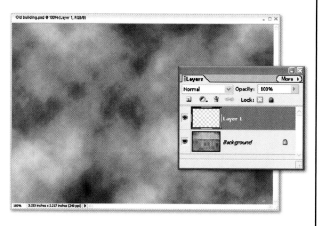

(3) Choose Filter⊏>Brush Strokes⊏>Spatter to apply the Spatter filter, dragging both the Spray Radius and Smoothness sliders to their maximum settings.

(4) Change the blend mode of the bottom layer (Layer 1) in the Layers palette to Overlay. Like all Blending modes, it affects how the pixels on the different layers interact and how the top layer appears to the viewer.

(5) The next characteristic of an old photo you need to duplicate is the cracking that sometimes appears in parts of the emulsion. Duplicate Layer 1 and change the blend mode to Normal. Apply Find Edges (Filter⊏> Stylize⊏>Find Edges) and then invert the layer (Ctrl+I). Apply Auto Levels (Shift+Ctrl+L) and Sharpen Edges (Filter⊏>Sharpen⊏>Sharpen Edges).

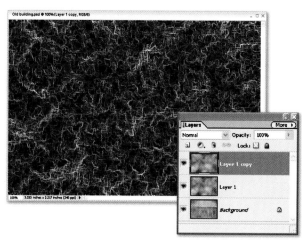

6 To simulate a greater amount of deterioration, set the blend mode of the top layer to Screen. Doing this increases the amount of fake damage. To make the effect of using this mode more realistic, change the Opacity of the top layer to 60%.

TIP

To lessen the appearance of damage, change the blend mode of the top layer to Lighten.

7 Next, add a paper matte, which is fitting for the period of time we are attempting to create, around the image. Select the Background by clicking on it and, using the Eyedropper tool (I), click on a light shade of brown on the metal porch roof. Use the Canvas Size command (Image⇨Resize⇨Canvas Size) to create a .75-inch border that has the new Foreground color you sampled from the roof.

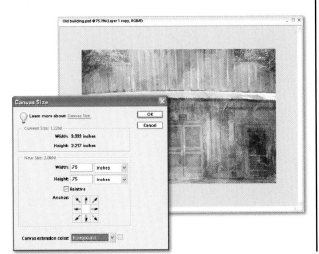

8 Whether old or new, the frame needs some treatment to make it appear real. The first step is to isolate it from the background. Here is a quick trick to create the perfect selection: In the Layers palette, hold down Ctrl and click on either of the two layer thumbnails. Elements creates a selection based on the layer transparency.

Ctrl-click either thumbnail to create a selection based on layer transparency

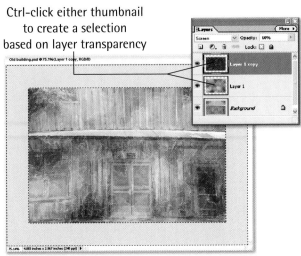

9 Invert the selection (Ctrl+Shift+I), then apply the Texturizer (Filter⇨Texture⇨Texturizer) to the frame. Set the texture to Burlap, Scaling to 100%, Relief to 1, and Light to Top.

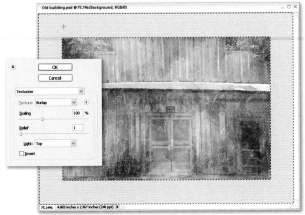

10 Press Ctrl+J to make the frame into its own layer. Elements names this layer Layer 2. From the Styles and Effects palette, apply a Low Drop Shadow and a Simple Inner Bevel to the layer. Double-click on the Styles icon shown, which opens the Style Settings adjustment box. Change the Shadow distance to 7 px and set Bevel Size to 4 px. Set the Bevel Direction option to Up. Make sure the Preview check box is selected.

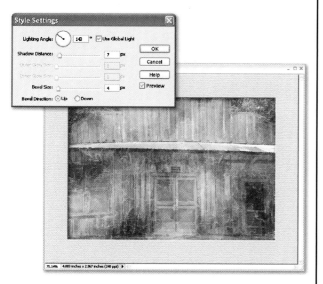

11 Reselect the frame as shown in Step 8. Press D to restore the foreground and background colors to the default settings. In the Layers palette, apply the Clouds filter (Filter⇨Render⇨Clouds...) and then the Ripple filter (Filter⇨Distort⇨Ripple...) at 300% to Layer 1.

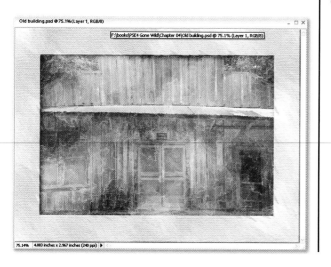

12 Photos often suffer additional damage. In the Layers palette, select the Background. Change the Foreground color to a dark coffee brown. Add a new layer above the layer that contains the frame. Choose the Custom Shape tool, select one of the crop shapes that looks like a splatter, and drag a shape in the corner so it looks like someone spilled coffee on the frame. Change the Opacity to 60% to make the splatter look more like an old stain.

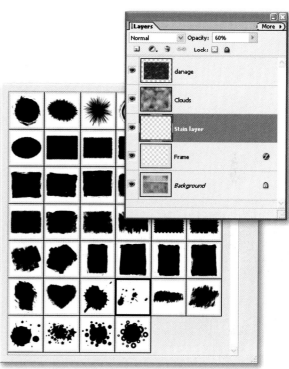

(13) Most of the old photos I have worked with have had something written on the frame or on the back, so to complete the illusion, I wrote some information using my Wacom tablet (couldn't do it with a mouse) on the layer containing the stain.

Late Night Church

For me there is something special about a building with light shining out of the windows at twilight. As a photographer, I seldom find the right combination of lighting and weather to get the shots I want, so it becomes necessary to create the lighting effects as well as the twilight sky myself. For this task, you use a photo I shot of an abandoned church in Nebraska and a custom gradient.

1 Open abandoned church.psd and make a copy of the Background into a layer by clicking and dragging the background in the Layers palette onto the Create New Layer icon in the Layers palette. Name this layer **Church** and then hide the Background.

2 Select the Magic Wand tool. With Tolerance set to 30 and both Anti-alias and Contiguous checked, select the overcast sky and then delete (Del) it. Deselect the selection (Ctrl+D) before creating a new layer.

3 Drag the new layer below the Church layer and label it **Twilight**. Hide the Church layer.

TIP

To create the twilight sky, you need the custom gradient twilight.grd, which you can download from the book's Web site, www.wiley.com/go/elementsgonewild. Copy twilight .grd to the folder \PROGRAM FILES\ADOBE\PHOTOSHOP ELEMENTS 4.0\GRADIENTS.

4 Select the Gradient tool and open the Gradient editor. In the dialog box click the Load button. Locate and load the Twilight gradient file; it should appear at the bottom of the presets. Select Twilight and then click OK. Select the Twilight layer and beginning at the top of the image, click and drag a straight line to the bottom as shown below.

5 To remove the appearance of banding, apply Motion Blur with an Angle setting of –90 degrees and a Distance setting of 150 pixels. To complete the sky we need to make the upper regions a little darker, select the Brush tool and with black as the foreground color, using a brush size of 350 px and an Opacity of 20%, paint the left and right edges of the sky as shown.

6 The church building and the foreground are still too well lit. Because the church and ground are dark, the colors should be cool. Select the Church layer, choose Filter⇨Adjustments⇨Photo Filter, and apply Cooling Filter (82) with Density set at 25%, Preserve Luminosity checked.

(7) Press Ctrl+L to open the Levels dialog box. Change the setting of the Output Level in the lower part of the dialog box to 0, 140.

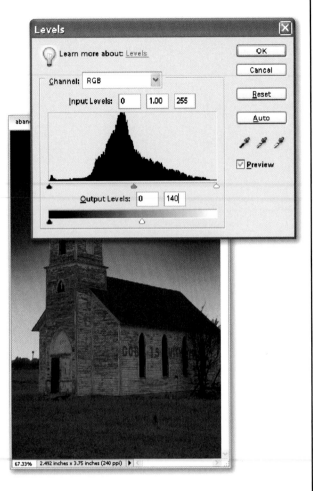

(8) Select the Twilight layer, change the Foreground color to white, and select the Brush tool. Change the brush Opacity to 100% and select a soft 5-pixel brush. Add a few stars to the sky by clicking a few spots in the upper darkness. Since it is supposed to be twilight and only the brightest stars can be seen, don't get carried away and add too many stars. Decrease the opacity to create some fainter stars.

TIP

When adding stars to a twilight or sunrise image, be aware that only the brightest stars are visible in the lighter portion of the sky and that more stars are visible in the darker portion.

(9) Select the Church layer in the Layers palette. Using the Burn tool set for Midtones at a 30% exposure, darken the area in the background of the church, and slightly darken the grass in front of the church as well as the steeple top and the roof. Now you have an abandoned church. Let's light it up.

(10) At this point, you can select all of the windows, dark openings, and even the closed door. Select the Gradient tool, change the Opacity setting to 90%, and in the Gradient Editor choose the other custom gradient (Windows). With the Church layer still selected, click-drag the cursor from the upper left to the lower right. Let there be light.

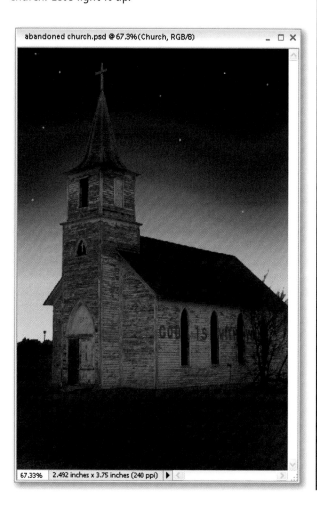

11 The remaining steps are about the finishing details. First, zoom in on the front door. It doesn't look very realistic, so you should fix it. The first step is to give the yellow rectangle some depth. Because the selection used in Step 10 is still loaded, use a small soft brush and a combination of dark brown and gold to create just the hint of shadows and possibly a floor inside the door jam.

12 It appears that there is no door on the left. Although an open-door policy is good, a no-door policy is not. Deselect the previous selection and use the Polygonal Lasso tool to select the door on the right. Create a layer (Ctrl+J) from that selection and move the new door over to the left as shown.

13 Apply a Perspective transformation (Image⇨Transform⇨Perspective) so that the door appears to be in the correct perspective for a left door, and paint it with a gold color at a low opacity; the door should appear to catch some of the light from the inside.

14 One last detail on the door: select the layer containing the new door and merge it with the Church layer. Create a new layer on top and label it **Lighting**. Create an elliptical selection in front of the door as shown. Use the Polygonal Lasso tool to expand the ellipse selection to the door.

15 With the Eyedropper, select the gold in the side windows and use the Brush tool at a low opacity to fill the selection as shown. Deselect the selection and apply a Gaussian blur at a setting of 14. Finally, apply a Perspective transformation to make the layer appear flat.

16 Select the Church layer and use the Magic Wand to select the windows on the side of the church. Apply slight shading on the right of each window as shown, similar to what was done on the doorway.

17 Now make some fake stained glass: Open the Glass filter (Filter⇨Distort⇨Glass) and apply the settings: Glass, Distortion: 3, Smoothness: 2, Texture: Frosted, Scaling 50%, Invert: unchecked. These brightly lit windows should be casting a small amount of light on the outside grass, so select the Lighting layer and using the Brush tool and the same color used for the light in front of the door paint a very light amount of soft light reflecting on the grass.

18 For the light coming from the bell tower, repeat a similar treatment as was done to create the light in the doorway. That's it.

Sports in Motion: Faking a Multiple Exposure

After you have captured an action scene with your digital camera, you enter a new world of digital manipulation that, up until now, has been limited to only those photographers who produce the fine art that appears on the covers of supermarket tabloids. Yes, with Elements and a little imagination, you too can create the extraordinary action photos that regale the covers of sports magazines and the British tabloids.

To demonstrate some of the things that are possible, meet my associate Paul. He is 12 and he is also 100 percent boy. The photo shown was taken right after church as he was working off all of the excitement that naturally builds up as you nap during the sermon.

① Open Skateboard.psd. The first job is to separate the skateboarder from the background. Use the Magic Extractor to remove all of the background, leaving the skateboarder floating around on a layer all by himself. Next, use the Canvas Size command to create a slightly larger background (Choose a size of 3 x 2 inches); because you are going to make an action photo, you want him to have plenty of room.

② First, you must flip the image to face the other direction. Open clouds.jpg and drag it onto the image. From the Layers palette, move the layer containing the skateboarder to the top.

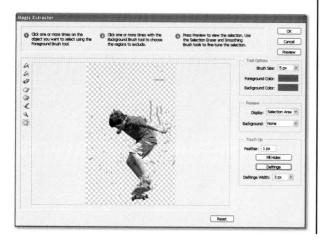

3 Duplicate the skateboarder three times by dragging the layer containing the skateboarder onto the Create a new Layer icon at the top of the Layers palette. You now have four skateboarders. Use the Move tool (V) to separate them as shown.

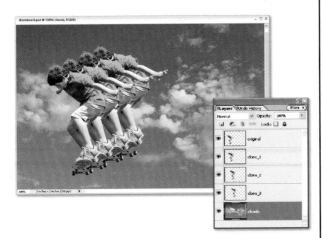

4 Select the bottom layer (clone_3). He will be the last skateboarder in the sequence. Move him away from the others. Rotate him back slightly to create the illusion that he is farthest away. You must also reduce his size slightly by dragging a corner handle inward towards the center.

5 Select the next higher layer (clone_2) and repeat Step 4 to making it smaller, but not as small as clone_3. Make the amount of rotation slightly different than clone_3.

6 Selecting the clone_1 layer, keep it the same size, rotate it slightly to the right, and after selecting Free Transform (Ctrl+T), right-click on the layer and choose Skew.

7 Drag the left handle upward to distort the shape so it looks less like the others.

8 In the Layers palette select the bottom skateboarders (clone_3) and change the Opacity to 70%. Then change the opacity of clone_2 to 80%.

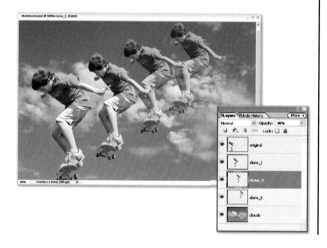

9 This last step adds a trailing blur to give the effect of speed. It is simple but it must be applied to all of the layers. Beginning with the bottom layer, duplicate the layer producing two identical images. To the bottom of the two images apply Motion Blur at an Angle of 30 and a Distance of 25 pixels. After the Motion Blur is applied use the arrow keys to move the blurred image so it can only be seen on the trailing edge.

10 Repeat on all of the other layers, and you're done.

Flower Power

When you open Photoshop Elements 4, the first photo that confronts you is that of a flower that appears to be six feet tall serving as a beach umbrella. If flowers grew that big (they do grow that big in Texas) or it had been a tree, it would have just been a nice photo. It is the impossiblity of it that causes most viewers to give it a second look. Creating these mismatched objects is easy and fun. In this task, I thought it symbolic to replace the propellors of a war plane with some flower petals, since back in the Sixties the opposition to the war in Vietnam referred to their power to change as "flower power." If you haven't heard about flower power, ask someone who is at least 60 years old and they can explain it. I choose the flower you use in this task because its center naturally looks smooth and polished. The petals are not uniform, but we can fix that. This task requires you to download the files flower.psd and fighter plane.jpg from www.wiley.com/go/elementsgonewild.

1 Open the photo flower.psd. To save you some time, I have already removed the background so that the flower appears isolated on its own layer.

2 To make the flower petals a little more symmetrical, you need to replace a few of the curled. Use the Magnetic Lasso tool and select one of the lower petals as shown. Once the petal is selected, copy it to its own layer (Ctrl+J) and name the layer **Petal 1**.

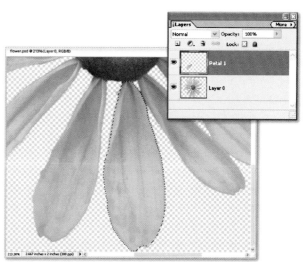

(3) Select the Move tool (V) and drag Petal 1 over to cover the original lower-left petal. Select Free Transform (Ctrl+T) and place the cursor outside of one of the corner handles until the cursor becomes a double-headed curved arrow. Drag the handle to rotate the petal as shown. Double-click the petal to apply the transformation.

(4) Make a copy of the Petal 1 layer. Move one of them (Petal 2) over to the lower-right as shown. In this case, the original petal can still be seen and the petal is out of perspective.

(5) To remove one of the original petals, turn off all of the Petal layers by holding down the Ctrl key and clicking on the eye icon of the Background in the Layers palette. Select the Eraser tool and remove the original petal as shown.

(6) Make Petal 2 layer visible again by clicking on the eye icon of its layer. The petal shape is not in perspective, so select the Move tool and evoke Free Transformation (Ctrl+T) and right-click on the petal. From the pop-up menu that appears choose Distort. Change the shape of the petal by dragging the handles until it has a shape that is more appropriate for the angle that it is being viewed.

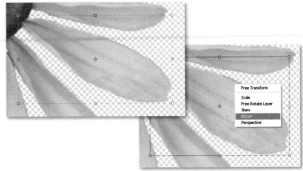

7 Make a copy of Petal 2 and label it Petal 3. Drag it up to cover the petal above the one that was just replaced. Rotate it and transform it until it looks as shown. Make sure all of the layers are visible and merge all of the layers together Layer⇨Merge Visible.

8 Open the file fighter plane.jpg and then use to Move tool to drag the flower layer onto this photo. Put the flower photo into the Photo Bin, because you'll need it in a minute.

9 Select the Move tool and move the flower layer over where the original propeller is located. It is completely out of perspective, so enable Free Transformation (Ctrl+T), right-click on the flower layer, and choose Perspective. Drag the lower-right corner upward until it looks as shown.

10 Open the Styles and Effects palette, and from the Drop Shadow category choose Hard. It will look really ugly when you do this, but be patient. In the Layers palette, double-click on the Layers icon and change the Shadow Distance to 1 pixel (px) and the Lighting Angle to 90 degrees.

11. With the flower layer selected, click the Lock transparency icon in the Layers palette. Using the Brush tool with 14% opacity, paint shadows and highlights on the propeller as shown.

12. As a finishing touch, from the Flower photo in the Photo Bin, drag the top layer onto the fighter plane just like it was done in step 8. Use transformation to make it appear to be painted on the tail of the aircraft as shown.

13 Complete the task by selecting the Type tool and giving the pilot a name underneath his cockpit. Change the Foreground color to white. In the Options bar select Lucida Handwriting at 6 points (pt); click the cursor anywhere in the image and type in the text **Flower Power**.

As with the petal and the flower layers, use the Move tool and change the perspective of the text so it appears to be painted below the cockpit as shown. Then, in the Layers palette, change the Blend mode of the text to Overlay, and you are done.

Alien Sky with Windmills

If there is a common site in the midwest, it is windmills. These tireless giants seem to be everywhere, which is one reason that they also are popular icons used in graphics in everything ranging from menus to Web sites. A small town in Texas wanted a unique treatment of this prairie icon for an upcoming festival, and this exercise shows what I made for them. I liked the effect, but the committee making the final decision thought it was too wild, so I thought I would share it with my readers in the form of a poster for a Windmill Tilting Festival. (The actual name of the town and the festival have been changed to protect the innocent.) For the record: we don't tip windmills in Texas, and we rarely tip cows. To complete this project, you need to download the photo Windmill.psd from www.wiley.com/go/elementsgonewild.

1 Open the photo Windmill.psd. In the Layers palette, make a copy of the Background. A quick way to make a copy of the background is to drag the background in the Layers palette on top of the "Create a new layer" icon near the top left of the palette.

2 Change the Blend mode of the copy to Multiply. The photo becomes darker.

TIP

Making a background copy of an image and changing the Blending mode to Multiply is a great way to darken a mildly overexposed image.

(3) Add a Gradient Adjustment Layer by choosing Layer⇨New Adjustment Layer⇨Gradient map. This command opens dialog box that allows you to give the Gradient Layer a name. Accept the default name. Next, the Gradient Map dialog box appears. Click on the down arrow to open the currently installed gradient maps. From the drop-down list, click the small options triangle button on the right opening of the Gradient options. Choose Large List and the options list will close. Open it again and choose Pastels.

(4) From the Gradient list select the gradient labeled Yellow, Pink, Purple and click OK. In the Layers palette, choose the Hue blending mode and the background is complete.

5 For the text of the poster, select the Type tool in the Tool palette and in the Options bar change the Font to Copperplate Gothic Bold at a size of 12 points (pt). Change the foreground color to white. Type in **2nd Annual Windmill Tilting Festival**.

6 With the text still selected, click the Create Warped Text icon in the Options bar to open the Warp Text dialog box. Change the Style to Rise, select the Horizontal option. Set Bend to 20%, Horizontal Distortion to 10%, and Vertical Distortion to –10%.

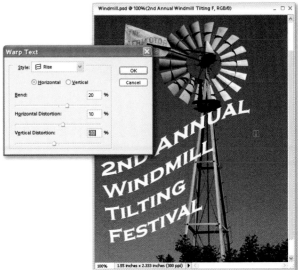

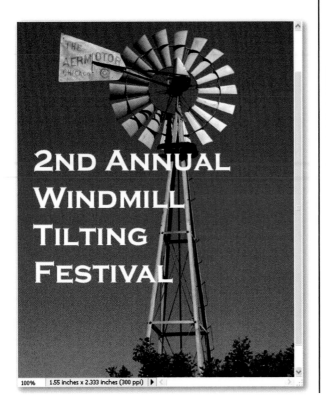

7 Open the Styles and Effects palette and from the Styles category pick Drop Shadows and double-click the Low preset.

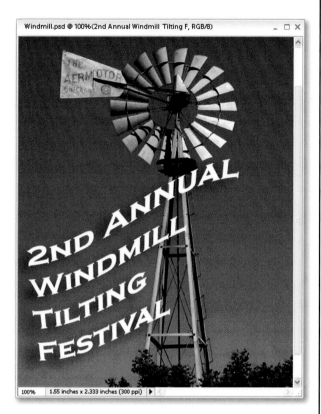

8 Complete the poster by adding the name of the town. Select the Type Horizontal tool, and change the font to Arial at a size of 7 points. Click on the image and type in **Windy Point, Texas**.

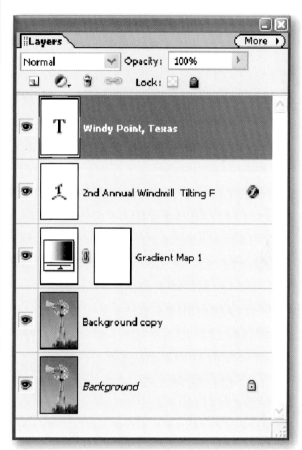

chapter

5

making photos into paintings

One of the first features people notice when beginning to explore Photoshop Elements is that it contains a lot of filters that appear to automatically convert photos into art. A majority of these filters are grouped into one of several filter categories: Artistic, Brush Strokes, Stylize, and Sketch. All of the artistic plug-ins in Photoshop Elements work by applying brush effects to an image to produce the desired painterly effect. The problem facing most users is that many of these brushes are a fixed size, so when the filter is applied to a large image, the brush-strokes the filter produces may be so small that the image may appear unchanged. Conversely, if you apply the same filter to a smaller image, such as one that you may have downloaded from the Internet, the filter's fixed brushes are now quite large by comparison, producing an effect that makes the image unrecognizable.

Because you cannot change the size of the effect brushes, you have to change the size of the image to fit the filters. This means making large images smaller or enlarging small ones. When the filter action is completed, the image can be restored to the original size by resizing once again.

Still-Life Masterpieces

Converting photos of people into images that appear to have been hand drawn or painted can be challenging, so this chapter begins by explaining how to convert still-life subjects into artistic-looking images. I begin with a photo of a church in a very small Texas town. I picked this image because, although the church structure has an appealing design, the entrance looks rather plain. Brown stairs, brown brick, brown...you get the idea. So, when the members of the church wanted to put a photo of the entrance on a welcome brochure, I thought that substituting a painting of the entrance might add some interest to the cover. Here's how to do it:

(1) Open the image Little brown church.psd (sorry, couldn't resist the name). The first step is to make two layer copies of the background in the Layers palette. Select the top layer and use Hue/Saturation (Ctrl+U) to increase the Saturation to +30. If you think that setting is excessive, you would be correct if we weren't making it into a drawing. After you have increased the saturation, make the top layer invisible.

(2) Select the top visible layer and apply Find Edges (Filter⇨Stylize⇨Find Edges). Next remove the color from the layer (Ctrl+Shift+U), make the top layer visible again, and change the Blending Mode of the top layer from Normal to Hard Light and you're done although there are some other changes you can make.

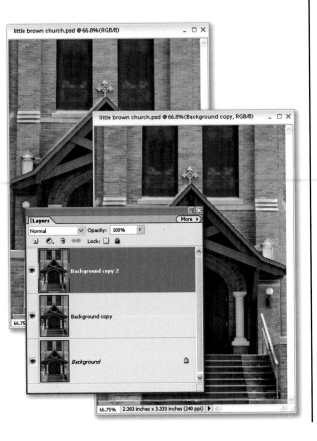

3) Here are some adjustments you can make at this point that will effect how the final image appears. The two major areas of adjustment involve how dark the lines in the final image appear, and how the colors appear. We'll begin with line darkness. In the Layers palette select the middle layer but keep all layers visible. Open Levels (Ctrl+L), and as you move the middle slider, watch how it affects the darkness of the lines in the painting. The examples show the original, the original with a gamma (middle setting) of 0.5, which makes the lines darker and brings out the detail, and the original again with a gamma setting of 0.20, which makes the image look like a panel from a dark comic book.

4 The choice of blending modes has a profound impact on the final appearance as well. There are so many blending modes (19) that I have shown just the ones that will be of the greatest use. The examples show the original with the Levels setting of the middle layer set to 0.5. Next is same image with the top layer set to Linear Light. This produces the greatest saturated color and enhances the illustration effect for any photo. Using Color Burn is pretty wild and I am sure this client wouldn't find it appealing.

5 For the finishing touch I used the Canvas command to extend the border and added the requested text. In case you were wondering, the client picked the final effect and the color of the text. The paying customer is always right.

Producing a True Watercolor Edge

When the original photo is large and has a lot of areas of uniform color, there is a different way to give it the appearance of a hand-drawn illustration. The image used in this exercise is a quite large (1000 x 1500 pixels) close-up photo of a Texas courthouse.

(1) Open courthouse.psd. I used the Canvas command to make a white border around the original photo. Apply the Watercolor filter using the settings shown. To better evaluate any filter settings, zoom in until the photo fills the preview area. Make two copies of the background and then use Fill Layer to make the background white.

(3) Select the bottom layer and add a Levels adjustment layer (Layer, New Adjustment Layer, Levels). Click OK to close the Name Layer dialog box, and when the Levels dialog box opens, push the left Output Levels slider on the bottom all of the way to the right and the image will disappear. Click OK and then group the adjustment layer to the image below it (Ctrl+G).

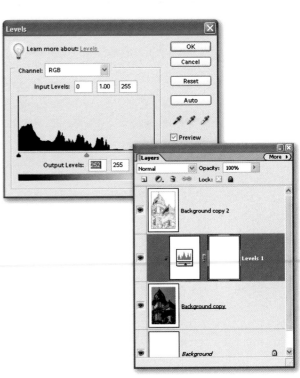

(2) Select the top layer and apply Find Edges and change the blending mode to Soft Light.

④ Now comes the fun part. Change the foreground color to black and choose one of the Wet Media brushes. I recommend the brush labeled Oil Medium Brush Wet Edges because it produces an edge that looks a lot like watercolors being absorbed into wet paper. Your technique at this point determines how painterly the finished image looks like. The goal is to give the viewer the impression that the courthouse was painted on the paper in a freeform style, so we don't want to reveal the straight edges of the original photo. You can use the top image as a guide by changing the Soft Light blending mode temporarily to Normal and reducing the layer opacity to 5%. Because the default opacity setting of the Oil Medium Brush Wet Edges is 50% opacity, it will lay down a gray stroke. Select the Adjustment Layer Mask thumbnail, and on the image begin by painting an overlapping zigzag from the top to the bottom without releasing the mouse button, as shown in the incomplete example below. Change the opacity to 80% and cover the same area again. I have included a shot of the completed image taken at 100% and also at Fit Screen so you can see the entire image. You can also control the lightness or darkness of the image by applying Levels changes on the bottom image.

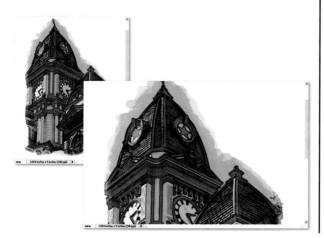

There are several different ways to use this watercolor effect. In the image below, I used the straight illustration technique from the beginning of the chapter, and instead of trying to achieve the blurred watercolor edge, I used a Wet Media brush to define the edges and then the Texturizer filter (Filter, Texture, Texturizer). To achieve the effect of a good quality art paper, I changed the setting to Burlap and made the scale 200%.

Here is another example of obtaining the illusion of watercolor by applying one of the many custom brushes included with Photoshop Elements to the clipping mask as we did in the previous task. The original photograph is one I took of some aquatic birds in Florida. By creating a clipping mask with the adjustment layer, as done previously, I applied the Oil Medium Brush Wet Edges at different opacity settings. By clicking on the thumbnail of the Adjustment Layer mask while holding down the Alt key, the image area fills with the brushstrokes applied to the layer mask as shown below. The result is a photograph that appears to be painted.

People Painting

Up until now, I have been showing how to convert only still-life or nature subjects into paintings, but in truth, most people want to change photos of people into paintings; so let's learn how to do that before we do anything fancier in the still-life/nature department. I begin by showing a quick and easy technique.

1 Open the image swabby.psd and increase the Saturation (Ctrl+U) by +30. The actual amount of saturation is determined by the saturation in the original image. The best method is to increase the saturation while viewing the image until the colors begin looking weird (oversaturated).

2 Make a copy of the background. Select the newly created layer and apply Glowing Edges (Filter⇨Stylize⇨Glowing Edges) using the settings shown. See the sidebar "Understanding Glowing Edges." Invert the top layer (Ctrl+I).

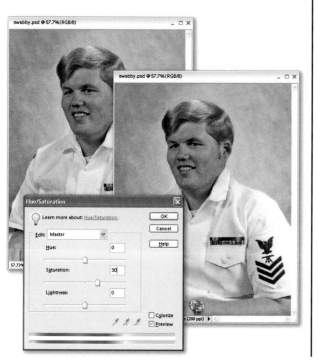

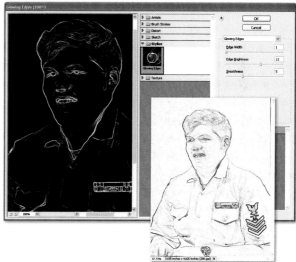

3 Change the blending mode of the layer to Overlay. At this point you can select the background and, using Levels, push the highlights of the image to give it a modern fashion-illustration appearance. I have included 100%-zoom (Actual pixels) shots of the original and after the Gamma in Levels was pushed to 1.8 (from 1.00).

Understanding Glowing Edges

The Glowing Edges filter is, at best, an obscure filter buried in a pantheon of other filters in Photoshop Elements. Most users try this filter once, scratch their heads and never use it again. For painterly effects, this filter is essential for creating the appearance of a hand-drawn outline, so it helps to understand what the three sliders do and how to adjust them to fit each image. The Edge Width slider controls the width of the edge that's produced. As the edges get wider they become more dominate, and detail in the image becomes exaggerated. In most cases, using a lower setting preserves tiny details in the image. Edge Brightness increases the overall brightness of the edges, and when used for painterly effects, it controls how dark the outlines in your image appear. Smoothness actually blurs the image and is great for smoothing out what can be hundreds of tiny artifacts when applying this filter to a high contrast image.

Master Image for Multiple Effects

Until now, all of the tasks in this chapter focus on producing a specific painterly effect. Blending modes create a wide range of effects when applied to either single or multiple layers. These effects are compounded when these blending modes are combined. This task is a little more complex than the previous one, but from a single image you can create many different effects by simply changing the blending modes.

(1) Open young woman in shadows.psd and copy the background to a layer.

(2) Select the top layer and apply the Poster Edges filter (Thickness: 0, Edge Intensity: 1, and Posterization: 6). Apply the effect by clicking the icon next to the trash can. Select Paint Daubs and change the setting to Brush Size: 7, Sharpness: 10, and a Simple Brush Type. Then click OK.

3 Select the top layer and change the blending mode to Linear Light, making most of the image too dark. Select the background and add a layer that sits between the background and the top layer. Use Fill Layer to fill it with a dark gray (R 60, G 60, B 60).

4 Apply the Brush tool to the new layer to make areas you want to lighten white and areas you want to darken black. See the sidebar "Painting for Highlights" for more information on how to get best effects at this stage. How this stage of the finished image should appear is one of personal choice. The image shown is how I wanted it to come out. Yours may be different.

Painting for Highlights

This is where a pressure-sensitive tablet comes in very handy. Most highlights are a result of light falling on the subject in a specific area. Highlights give an image a sense of depth. Some highlights (specular) are bright reflections, as from a flash or other bright light reflecting off of the subject's face. When changing a photo into a painting, try and maintain highlights. You may not want to remove specular highlights but instead use the paintbrush to soften their appearance.

5 After you are satisfied with the highlights and shadows, merge the layers. Duplicate the layer and apply Find Edges to the top layer and then remove the color (Ctrl+Shift+U). At this point you have the basic image from which you can create a number of different looks with only one or two keystrokes. To get a look that was very popular in the '60s, change the blending mode to Vivid Light (Color Dodge and Hard Mix are both alternatives). Color Burn makes the image appear darker. Applying a halftone pattern to the top layer and changing the blending mode to Multiply is another variation.

6 The lines of the top layer can look strange on her face when viewed with a lighter blending mode. Place a layer mask between the top two layers to prevent the lines from occurring on the subject's face (they look fine everywhere else).

Getting the Lead Out

If you are working with images that need to be put into a single- or two-color project, that is a good time to create the effect of a pencil drawing. There is something really cool about a photo that appears to have been drawn and shaded with a lead pencil. Achieving this effect requires using one of the many artistic plug-ins included in Photoshop Elements.

(1) Open Bruce.psd, create a duplicate layer, and then make the top layer invisible. With the bottom layer selected, make sure the foreground color is white and the background color is black.

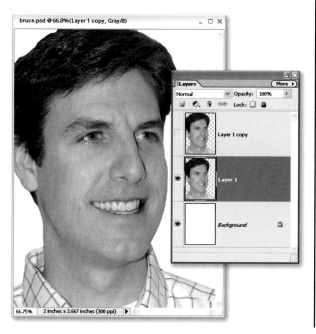

(2) Open the Chalk & Charcoal filter (Filter⇨Sketch⇨ Chalk & Charcoal). While in this dialog box, we are going to apply two filters. Change the settings for Chalk & Charcoal as shown. The key to this effect is the Stroke Pressure slider. As you move it to the right it hits a threshold, causing areas of the photo to quickly become much whiter. When that happens, move the slider back to the left until the bright white goes away. That's the setting you want. Don't click OK yet. Instead click the icon next to the trash can (bottom right) and then select the Halftone Pattern filter. Use a size of 1 and the Line Pattern Type. Use a low overall Contrast setting as shown. Now you can click OK.

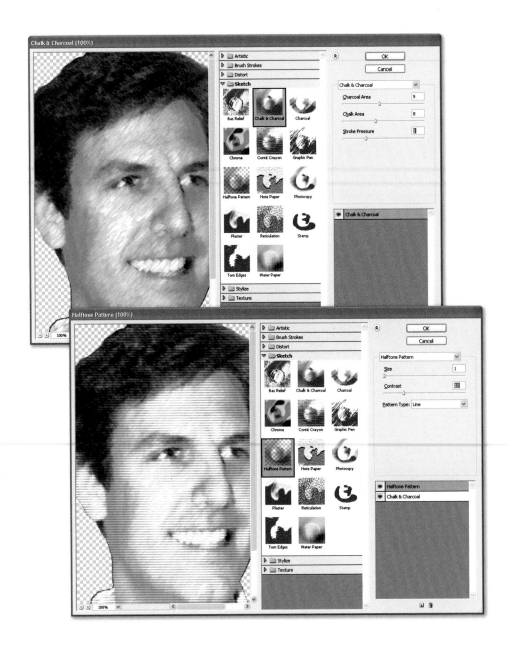

3 Make the top layer visible and then change the blending mode to Hard Light, which makes quite a difference.

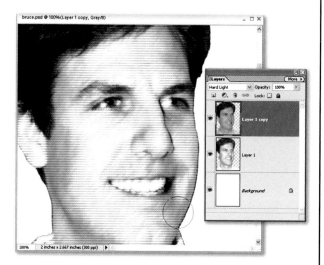

4 At this point you have several choices in how you want to create the appearance of a hand-drawn pencil sketch. All of them use the bottom layer as the working layer. With the bottom layer selected, you can use the Smudge tool to smudge all of the lines produced by the Halftone filter so they appear to be shadows. Set the Opacity at around 15% and enable the Finger Painting options in the Options bar. Use up and down strokes that are perpendicular to the lines made by the Halftone filter. This approach is time consuming but produces the best results. To speed up the process, apply Gaussian Blur at a setting of 3 pixels.

5 To complete the sketch, the ear needs fixing. The area was too bright and it now has little or no detail. Select the Brush tool and change the foreground color to black. With Opacity set to 25%, use the brush to paint over the ear on the working layer. The detail becomes more apparent.

6 Bruce's hair has a salt-and-pepper appearance, which is lost when converting it to a pencil sketch. To correct this, select the top layer, change the foreground color to white, and with an Opacity setting of 10% paint the hair, making the white in his hair stand out more. You can also apply it to the slightly dark spot under his nose. Finally, select the working (lower) layer and apply Levels (Ctrl+L) to it, adjusting the darkness of the shading as shown.

7 The last optional touch is to add a paper background using a pattern Fill Layer. I recommend Watercolor. Merge the two layers so there is only one layer above the background. Change the blending mode to Linear Burn and that's it.

A Different Approach to Making Watercolors

Photoshop Elements includes a lot of painterly effect plug-ins that in some situations can make short work of converting photos into paintings. This works exceptionally well when the subject matter is well defined and has simple lines. In this task, you recover lost detail in an image as you make it into a painting.

1 Open the image old barn.psd. Because the sky was bright and overcast, the image appears washed out in the photo. The cloud detail is there and should be recovered. Apply a Levels adjustment layer (Layer⇨New Adjustment Layer⇨Levels) and accept the default name. In the Levels dialog box, move the right (highlight) slider to the left to the rectangular-shaped spike on the right side of the histogram, and move the middle (gamma) slider to the right side of the spike.

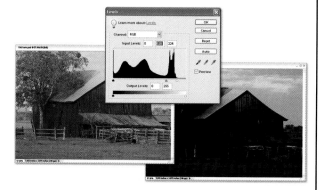

2 The sky looks great but the rest of the image is too dark. So, select the Layer Mask thumbnail in the Layers palette and then select the Brush tool (B). Begin painting everywhere on the image that you want to remove the effect of the adjustment layer. Everywhere on the image that you paint black removes the adjustment layer darkness. If you make a mistake, change the color to white and paint over the same area to undo it.

Text Only
Small Thumbnail
✔ Large Thumbnail
Small List
Large List

All Elements Shapes
Animals
Animals2
Arrows
Banners and Awards
Characters
✔ Crop Shapes
Default
Dressup
Face
Flowers
Foliage and Trees
Food
Frames
Fruit
Music
Nature
Objects
Ornaments
Shapes
Signs
Symbols
Talk Bubbles
Tiles

3 Right-click on the adjustment layer and choose Flatten image, making the recovered sky part of the image so that the Watercolor filter can affect it. Choose and duplicate the background layer. Right-click on the new layer and choose Duplicate Layer. Many of these painterly effects require multiple layers. I advise that you keep the original or the starting image as the Background so you can use it at a later date.

4 In the Layers palette, select the background copy and choose Filter⇨Artistic⇨Watercolor. This opens a monster dialog box that fills the screen. On the left is a preview of the effect at 100% (best way to view it). On the far right are three sliders. You should experiment with these sliders to see what effects you like best. The Shadow Intensity slider controls the darkness of the image. Unless you have an overly bright image, leave it at 1. Brush Detail works the opposite of how you expect it to work. The higher the number, the less the effect. A setting of 8 or 9 is a good starting point. Texture is the slider that has the greatest effect on the image. It's range is 0–3. For this image I recommend a setting of 2.

TIP

When changing the slider settings, make sure you wait a moment for the image in the preview window to redraw so that you can see the effect of the setting change.

NOTE

The next step creates the illusion that the image is painted on a textured surface. If you are going to print this image on a paper media, then you shouldn't do this last step because the paper has its own texture.

5 When you have the sliders set the way you want them, click OK. The best way to evaluate any image in Photoshop Elements is at 100% zoom level (Ctrl+Alt+O); Adobe calls this Actual Pixels. You can enhance the watercolor illusion by making the image look like it was painted on some type of canvas or heavy paper, which traditionally has a coarse weave. For this we need the Texturizer, which sounds like the name of a '50s sci-fi thriller. Choose Filter⇨Texture⇨Texturizer. When the Texturizer dialog box opens, you see a drop-down list of textures. Although Canvas is one of the choices, choose Burlap, as it looks the closest to actual watercolor paper. Next, move the Scaling slider to 200% and keep the Relief slider at a setting of 3 or less. The Light and Invert box have little effect, so ignore them.

Creative Media Choices

As the versatility of inkjet printers continues to improve, so do the choices for media on which to print your masterpiece. To really make an image appear to be hand drawn, print it on a custom art paper. Many are unaware of the vast selection of papers — besides photo glossy — that are available. Here is just a sampling: Watercolor paper in multiple weights and textures, canvas, museum matte, and many more. Not all printers can use these art papers, but most professional-quality inkjet printers can, and the paper manufacturers maintain detailed lists of printers that are compatible with their papers.

Earlier in the chapter we learned that the natural media used in hand-drawn art produces an uneven-looking texture. Using a Layer Mask we discovered how to mimic that effect. Now you will learn a quick and dirty way to produce a similar unevenly stroked edge that further increases the illusion of a painting.

6 Select the background layer in the Layers palette. Open the Fill Layer dialog box (Edit⇨Fill Layer). Select the pattern called Watercolor in the collection labeled Artist Surfaces and apply it to the background. Other than in the Layers palette, the image appears unchanged.

7 Select the top layer in the Layers palette and then select the Cookie Cutter tool in the Toolbox. In the Options bar, choose one of the custom shapes. Adobe has a lot of preset shapes in Elements. To see all of the shapes

that are available for cropping, open the Options button and select Crop Shapes. I also used Large Thumbnails so I could see the approximate shape that I wanted. Click and drag the shape over the image as shown. You can use the handles to adjust the edges after you let go. Double-click on the shape to apply the Cookie Cutter shape.

8 For a final touch, select the background, apply the Texturizer to it (Ctrl+F), and flatten the image. I have included crops made with several of the many shapes included in Elements.

Here is something else you can try: The shapes that the Cookie Cutter uses can be transformed like any other shape. In the next example, I used a shape that I liked but that has a portrait rather than a landscape orientation. By using the Transform tool (Ctrl+T), I rotated the shape and distorted it a little before applying it to the image.

Airbrush Art

Images painted with an airbrush are unique in that the airbrush can produce smoother transitions than would be possible with any other media. This task is really simple but it doesn't work on every type of photo. In my limited experimentation, I find that it works best on subjects with large areas of light colors.

(1) Open the file youngwoman.psd. Make a copy of the background as a layer. In the Layers palette, select the background and choose the Fill Layer (Edit⇨Fill Layer), making black the fill layer. The background is now black but the image appears unchanged.

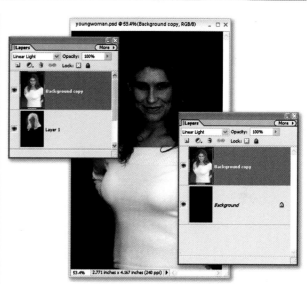

(3) Continue highlighting and darkening by applying either white or black to the background. Remember that you can change the opacity of your brush to control how much lighter or darker the image is.

(2) Select the top layer and change the blend mode to Linear Light. Now the image has changed dramatically. Select the background and choose the Brush tool. Change the foreground color to white and begin painting on the background where you want to bring out the original photo as shown.

4 Merge the top layer with the background. Select the black in the image and make a new layer via copy (Ctrl+J). Use Fill Layer to make the background white. The completed image is shown.

Colored Pencil Drawing

Photoshop Elements has an outstanding collection of built-in filters that were once sold separately under the name Gallery Effects. I have worked with these jewels for years. The next two tasks use some of my favorite tricks to kick Photoshop Elements' built-in painterly effect filters into high gear. Let's go.

Most users are disappointed when they try the Colored Pencil filter the first time. Here is how to make it work wonders for you.

1. Open the file new_orleans.psd. Make a copy of the background and apply the Colored Pencil filter (Filter, Artistic, Colored Pencil). The secret to making the background of this filter appear white is to push the Paper Brightness slider all of the way to 50. Apply the settings shown.

2 Make another copy of the background into a layer and then move the layer to the top. Apply Glowing Edges using the settings shown. Invert the layer (Ctrl+I) and desaturate the layer (Ctrl+Shift+U). Change the layer blending mode to Soft Light.

3 The last step is to make yet another copy of the background and drag it to the top of the Layers palette. Change the layer blending mode to Hard Light. That's it.

Faded Poster Print

Here is another jewel you can use to create a old faded poster print. Rather than make a photo look like an old photo, the goal in this task is to make the image look like it was printed as a poster that was exposed to general wear and tear for a lengthy period of time. If you've ever looked through your grandparents' photo albums, you'll know exactly the intended effect.

1. Open the image old truck.psd. Increase the saturation (Ctrl+U) to 40.

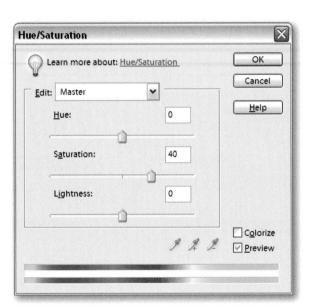

2. Duplicate the background and then make the new top layer invisible. Select the background and apply the Cutout filter (Filter➪Artistic➪Cutout) as shown.

3 Make the top layer visible. Apply the Glowing Edges filter (Filter➪Stylize➪Glowing Edges) and change the settings as shown. Invert the layer (Ctrl+I) and change the blending mode to Soft Light.

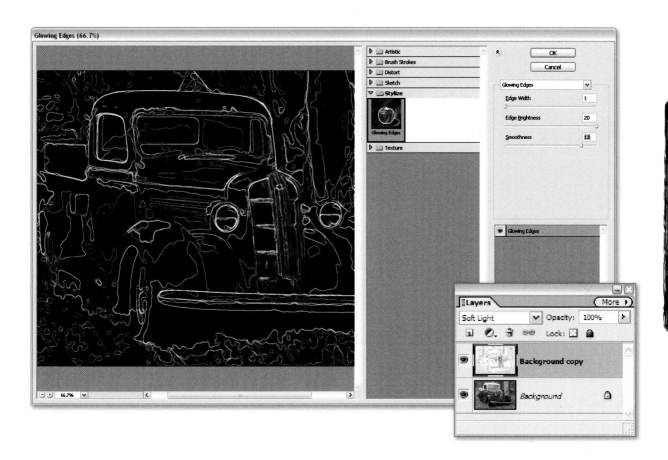

4 There are some cool variations possible at this point. First, flatten the image and then duplicate the remaining layer. Change the blending mode on the layer to Multiply to create a darker, richer image. Or, add a new layer, fill it with Clouds (Filter, Render, Clouds), and then change the blending mode to Soft light. The last variation puts Fibers into the layer instead of clouds and uses the Soft Light blend to give the appearance that the sign is weather streaked.

wild art effects

Murphy's Law affects graphic design as well as any other discipline. If you have the perfect photo, the surroundings are wrong. When you need a specific background, you can't find the one that you want. This chapter covers a wide variety of effects that either replace the surroundings of your photo, change the reality of an image, or transfrom new objects or scenes using existing photos or the tools within Elements.

Change My World

Keeping your camera at the ready allows you to capture moments that can never be recreated. Oftentimes the surroundings of these priceless pictures don't add to the overall composition, and at times they even detract from it. Most of the techniques described in this task are pretty basic stuff, but when used together effectively, they produce effects so realistic that, without the original, you can sometimes forget where the picture was actually taken.

1 Open the image Baby and blanket.jpg. The first thing you need to do is correct the blue color cast.

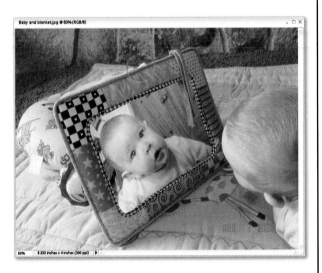

2 In Elements 4, bring up the Adjust Color for Skin Tone dialog box by clicking Enhance⇨Adjust Color⇨Adjust Color for Skin Tone. To correct the color cast, click the Eyedropper on the baby's forehead in the mirror.

3 Using your selection tool of choice, select the baby and the blanket. I used the Magic Selection brush to define the edges and completed the selection with the Rectangular Marquee tool. Add a 1-pixel feather (Select⇨Feather) and then convert the selection into a layer (Ctrl+J). Make the original Background invisible.

5 Open Sky.jpg and use the Move tool to drag the image onto the baby picture. Close Sky.jpg.

4 The background in the mirror shows that the photograph was taken indoors, so we need to replace it with a photograph of a blue sky. You can again use your favorite selection tool to select the background, but because it is so cluttered, just use the Magic Wand to select the major areas and then the Selection Brush to fine-tune the selection. Remove the reflection in the mirror using the Delete key. Delete the selection.

6 Use the Transformation (Image⇨Transform⇨Free Transform...) to change the general shape of the mirror's sky background as shown. The object is for the sky to have the same general shape of, and to be slightly larger than, the opening of the mirror.

7 Double-click the sky to apply the transformation. To complete the action, drag the sky so it is beneath the mirror.

8 The background that the blanket is laying on can be almost anything. If you live in Texas, it needs to be bluebonnet flowers; even though this young boy doesn't live in Texas, I like bluebonnets. Open the file flowers.jpg and drag the flowers onto the baby image.

9 Next, drag the flower layer so that it is above the Background and position it as shown.

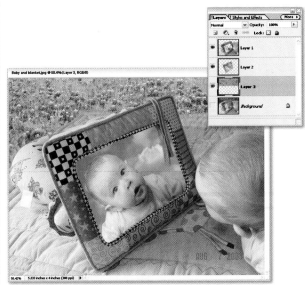

10 Your last step is to get rid of the date stamp. Select the top layer (baby and blanket) and use the Rectangular Marquee tool to create a rectangle with a 1-pixel feather. Select the Move tool (V) and, while holding down the Alt key, drag the selection over part of the date. Let go of the mouse button while still holding down the Alt key. The contents of the selection covers the date. Continue holding the Alt key and drag the selection over the remaining portions of the date stamp.

11 If you are a perfectionist, you may want to also remove the dark area on the blanket under the baby, which is obviously drool. Babies drool, it's a fact of life. Leave it. As a final touch, you can use the Levels command (Ctrl+L) and move the middle slider to make the sky brighter in the mirror. Select the layer containing the sky and use Levels to make the sky slightly brighter. That's all there is to it.

Signs of the Times

Signs are everywhere. There are signs on the roads, buses, cabs, buildings — just about any structure that has space for a sign has a sign on it. Most of us visually tune out these signs, but they can also be a source of great fun. While this book was being written, increasing gasoline prices dominated the headlines. I have seen many variations of the following technique, but regardless, it is great fun to create fake signs that look real enough to get a second look. The following task shows how to change a sign whose letters appear at an angle.

1 Open the image Gas price.jpg. The photo was taken on a bright overcast day which made the background almost pure white.

2 Select the Text tool and type the replacement name for the sign. You should not paint over the old sign, as you need the original lettering to serve as a guide. Here I chose a font that was closest to the original: Eras Demi ITC at 18 points.

TIP

If the image being created is for publication and public display, be sure to change to company's name for legal reasons. You don't want to be sued for trademark infringement.

TIP

Before doing anything else, take a moment to enjoy the photo. This photo has not been manipulated. It is a very real station sign in Texas taken in 2001. Sigh.

③ Use Transformation (Ctrl+T) to skew and rotate the text so that it aligns with the original. After it is aligned, select the background and use the Lasso tool to select the original text. Use the Eyedropper to get a color that matches the color behind the text and then paint over the text.

④ Place the new text over the painted area.

⑤ Remove the selection (Ctrl+D). Simplify the text, and then in the Layers palette check the Lock option. The black in the letters is too dark. Change the foreground color to a dark shade of gray and paint over the letters.

6 Because the price of gas changes so quickly, you need to change what is displayed in the number area. Use the Polygonal Lasso tool and outline one of the number rectangles as shown.

7 Select the layer containing the rectangle (gas sign). With the Eyedropper, select the color that matches the number board. Use the Brush tool to paint over the first number.

8 Select the Move tool (V), and while holding down the Alt key drag over the next number panel and let go. Continue until all of the numbers (not the fractions) are covered. Delete the selection (Ctrl+D).

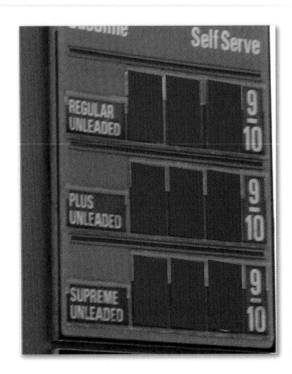

(9) Repeat Steps 6 to 8 to cover the fractions.

(10) Select the Text tool and create the replacements for the numerals. To recreate the example shown, use Impact font at a size of 27 points. Also, put one space between each letter to make the spacing work. After the text is in place, you will need to use the Skew option of Transformation to align the text as shown.

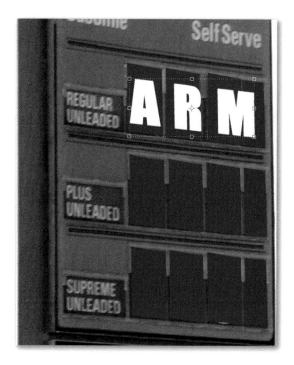

(11) The fastest way to add the two other price fillers is to duplicate the text layers and drag each duplicate into position on the sign. After the text is in position, you can change the letters as shown. The last layer required an extra word, so I changed the size of the text and then stretched it out to fit the area.

(12) Because we changed the name of the company to Cashgon, we should also change the colors of the chevrons; yes, the arrow shapes are called *chevrons*. Use the Magic Wand tool to select the top chevron and Hue/Saturation to change the colors. Repeat with the second chevron.

(13) Next, we need to make the very white new text we added look like the rest of the text on the sign. The quickest way to do this is in the Layers palette. Select all of the text, simplify it, and then merge the layers. Turn on the Lock option of the merged text layers. Use the Eyedropper to sample the color of the text (which is a very light blue) and then paint the text.

14 The finishing touch is to add a real sky background. The fastest way to do that is to flatten the image, use the Magic Wand tool to select the background, invert the selection (Ctrl+Shift+I), and make it into a layer (Ctrl+J). Finally, open a photo of the sky and place it behind the sign.

Size Is Relative

To live in Texas is to hear about how everything is bigger in the Lone Star state. It's not, but that's what we say. So, how big is bigger? It is all about comparision. We have expectations that some objects are a particular size in relationship to other objects. A dime is smaller than a car, and a moose is larger than a dog. In the movie *The Lord of the Rings,* the actors playing the hobbits appear to be half the height of the other actors, even though in real life all the actors were of similar heights. With Elements, you can change these size relationships, which can produce arresting results. I often see composite images made from cutting and pasting together separate pictures, and they look fake. This example shows you how to create realistic-looking changes in size relationships.

① Open Young woman standing.psd and Monument.psd, both of which are available from the book's Web site.

② The young woman was selected from the original photo using the Magic Extractor (Elements 4). It took almost 15 minutes to get an accurate selection, so to make this task a little easier, I provided her already selected and ready to go. Click and drag her onto the photo of the Washington Monument and then close Young woman standing.psd

3 Your next step is to wrap her hand around the top of the obelisk. In preparation, use the Move tool (V) and position her hand as shown.

6 Using the layer mask, you want to make the woman's hand appear to grasp the top of the obelisk. To create the illusion, you need to hide the parts of the hand that would not be visible if they really were behind the marble cap. In the Layers palette, select the Layer Mask thumbnail. Change the colors to the defaults (D) and paint with the Brush tool over the parts of the image that you do not want to show. Wherever you paint black on the image (with Layer Mask selected) disappears and wherever you paint white reappears.

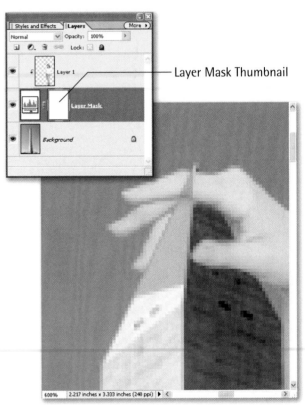

Layer Mask Thumbnail

4 Next, create a Layer Mask. In the Layers palette, select the Background. Add a Levels adjustment layer (Layer⇨New Adjustment Layer⇨Levels). When the dialog box opens, label the adjustment layer *Layer Mask*.

5 After you click OK, the Levels dialog box appears. Leave it unchanged and click OK. Select the top layer (Layer 1) and group it (Ctrl+G) with Layer Mask. You just made a layer mask.

7 Switch between black and white by pressing the X key. It isn't easy to paint a straight line, so I recommend using the Polygon Lasso tool to define the edges of the monument cap, indicated by the red selection mask. The finished hand is shown below.

8 Apply the same technique to the woman's feet, remembering that her legs are behind the higher row of flags and in front of the lower row of flags in back. To make the bluish flagpoles stand out, I used the Pencil tool and made them darker. At this point, we have the hand wrapped around the obelisk and her feet inside the flagpoles.

9 Notice that the sun is shining on the left side of the monument, making the right side dark. The model, on the other hand, was fully illuminated by a flash when her photo was taken. To further the illusion that she is in the same light as the monument, we need to create a shadow that would be cast if the sun were in the upper

left of the image (which it was in the monument photo). Using the Polygonal Marquee tool, create an oblique triangle like the one shown, using a feather of 2 pixels in the Options bar.

10 Select the layer containing the woman. Open the Levels command (Ctrl+L) and drag the middle slider to the right to darken it. Deselect the selection.

11 Her right side is still too brightly lit. The best way to achieve a soft shadow with either a mouse or a stylus is to make sure that the layer she is on is locked (this keeps all of the transparent pixels on the layer transparent). Then, using a large soft brush, allow just the edge of the brush to touch the area you want to shadow. The resulting shadows are soft and subtle.

12 To finish up, add some text, rotate it, and add a Low Drop Shadow from the Styles and Effects palette.

Twisted Steel

Often the starting point for a design can be something that is anything but exotic. When I was looking for a pattern to use for the background of a science fiction cover, I found what I was looking for in a series of photos I took of some rusted flywheels in an old Nebraska garage. This project uses several filters and a lot of filpping and rotating, plus a photo of lightning to achieve the desired effect.

(1) Open Flywheel.jpg and apply the Polar Coordinates filter (Filter⇨Distort⇨Polar Coordinates). Choose the Rectangular to Polar option and click OK.

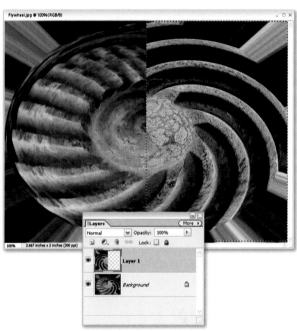

(2) Use the Rectangular Marquee tool (M) to select the right half of the image. Make the selection just slightly smaller than half. This prevents a seam in the composition. Convert the selection to a layer (Ctrl+J) and flip the layer horizontally (choose Image⇨Rotate⇨Flip Layer Horizontal).

(3) Move the new layer to the left side of the image and flatten the image.

169

In case you're wondering, the following image shows what the results would have been if you had copied and flipped the other side. From this starting point, you can make a large variety of images.

4 With the Elliptical Marquee tool, start at the center of the image and, while holding down the Alt key, drag out a circle whose shape is like the one shown. I have displayed it as a selection mask to make it easier to see; yours will just have a selection marquee. Convert the selection to a layer (Ctrl+J). Make Layer 1 invisible and select the Background.

5 Apply the Radial Blur filter (Filter➪Blur➪Radial Blur) at the settings shown.

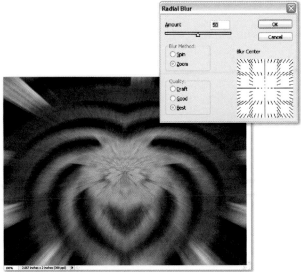

6 Select the top layer (Layer 1) and make it visible again. Use the Eraser tool to remove the portions of the top layer that intersect with the strong solid areas of the background. The goal is to make it look like power behind the layer is bursting through the top layer.

7 Use the Elliptical Marquee tool, create a small selection as shown, beginning at the center of the image while holding down the Alt and Shift keys. A light blue selection mask allows you to see the size and position of the selection more clearly than the typical marching ants marquee display.

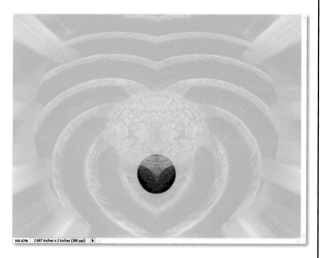

8 After you have the circle selection in the center, make a layer from it (Ctrl+J). Apply the WOW-Plastic Clear layer style from the Styles and Effects palette. Flatten the image. Lastly, rotate the image to the left (Image⇨Rotate⇨90 degrees Left)

9 Select the entire image (Ctrl+A) and make a new layer from the selection. Flip the layer horizontally. Now we need to make room for the new layer. Use the Canvas size command (Image⇨Resize⇨Canvas Size...) using the settings shown to double the width of the image.

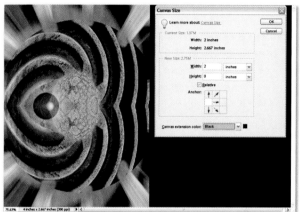

10 Drag the flipped top layer to the right side and flatten the image.

11 Open lightning.psd, a photograph of a great branched lightning strike from which I have already removed nonessential portions of the original image. Drag the layer onto the image you are creating and then close lightning.psd. Resize the lightning layer so it fits as shown, and then change the blending mode to Hard Light. This exposes the background, so use the Eraser tool to remove portions of the lightning background — but not all of it. The resulting image should appear as shown.

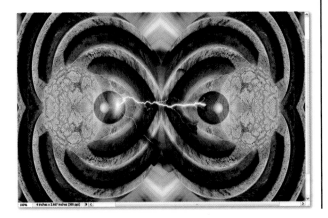

12 Use the Brush tool to apply a dark color to the lighter areas under the balls so it blends in better with the background. Add a Lens flare to each ball to finish the image.

Going Oriental

This project is a quick tour de force that takes the shape tools for a spin, showing just how much can be done with these little wonders. In this task, you create a basic metal shape and then transform it into a more complex shape. Then, you duplicate it many times before finally adding additional touches that make the shape look like an oriental display box.

1 Create a new 600-x-600-pixel image that has a white background. Choose the Custom Shape tool and select the custom shape shown in the figure. Drag a shape in the middle of the image window.

2 Duplicate the shape and make it invisible by clicking the eye icon in the Layers palette. Apply the WOW-Chrome Reflecting layer style to the bottom shape in the layers palette.

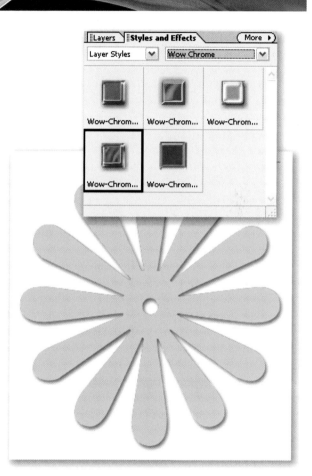

3 Make the top layer visible and using the Color Picker, change the foreground color with the color shown and use the Paint Bucket tool to fill it. Changing the blend mode to Color gives you the color and effect you want for your starting point. Merge the two layers together.

4 Duplicate the basic shape created in Step 1. Select the top layer and rotate the top shape while holding down the constrain (Shift) key. The duplicate layer will jump in 45-degree increments. Rotate this layer until it looks like the one shown. Double-click the image to apply the transformation. Merge these two layers together.

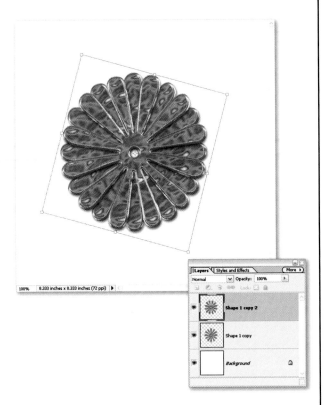

5 Duplicate the combined layer and resize the duplicate layer (on top) to be slightly smaller than the bottom layer. Use the Hue slider of the Hue/Saturation (Ctrl+U) dialog box to change the color of the top layer as shown. Merge these two layers together.

6 Here is how to make a pearl for this golden flower. Drag a small circle selection on the image while holding down the Shift key to keep the circle symmetrical. Make this selection into a layer (Ctrl+J). With the new layer selected, apply the WOW-Plastic White layer style. Position the pearl in the center before merging the two layers.

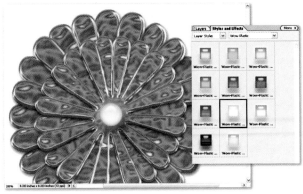

7 Turn on the Grid. You may need to open the Preferences and change the Grid settings to 1 grid space per 100 pixels. Resize the metal flower so it fits into a 200-x-200-pixels space. Duplicate the layer twice and distribute each layer as shown. Merge the three layers into one and then duplicate that layer. Position the resulting layer as shown. Continue to merge and group until you have covered the entire image.

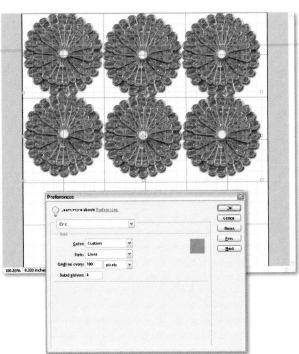

chapter 6 ● wild art effects

8 After you have a background like this, you can use it for all kinds of projects. In the example shown, the background is a little darker and the pearls are pink by request. The word *Japan* is created using text with a bevel layer style. The gold Japanese characters are also custom shapes to which the same gold treatment as in Step 1 was applied. The Glow is an Outer Glow layer style.

Heavy Metal Butterfly

A popular form of an optical illusion is to make natural objects appear to be made out of man-made or synthetic materials. The secret to the effect is creating the illusion that the shape being used has 3D characteristics. In this task we make use of the Cookie Cutter tool to create a myriad of shapes from photos of common ordinary materials with some surprising results. To complete this task, you need to download the files Hammered metal.jpg and Wall.jpg from www.wiley.com/go/elementsgonewild.

1 Open the photo Hammered metal.jpg. This is a photo of an old metal table top I saw in the junk shop.

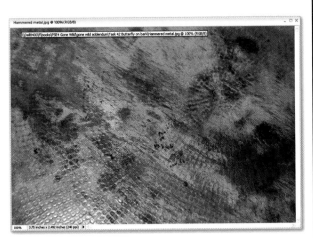

2 The first step is to select a shape to use for the task. Select the Cookie Cutter Tool (Q) in the Tools palette. In the Options bar, open the Shape drop-down list and select Butterfly 2.

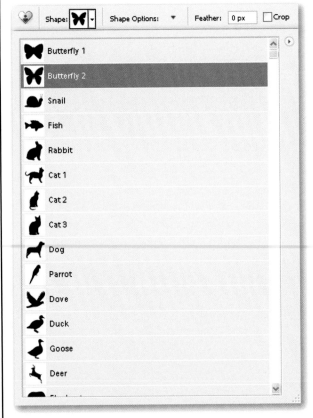

3 Hold down the Shift (constrain) key and, beginning in the upper-left corner of the image, drag the butterfly until the top and bottom edges of the shape are close to the top and bottom of the image as shown. Make sure you release the mouse button before releasing the Shift key. As soon as you release the mouse button, all of the photo that is outside of the shape is removed. Press the Enter key to complete the Cookie Cutter action, which makes the shape into a layer.

4 In the Layers palette, Ctrl-click the thumbnail of the butterfly layer to create a selection of the shape.

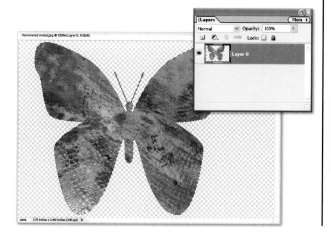

5 At this point, you must save the selection you created for use later in the task. Choose Select➪Save Selection, opening the Save Selection dialog box. Name the selection Butterfly and click the OK button. Delete the selection on the image (Ctrl+D).

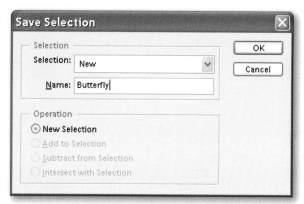

6 Open the Styles and Effects palette (Window ➪ Styles and Effect) and click on the Simple Emboss preset in the Bevels category of the Layer Styles.

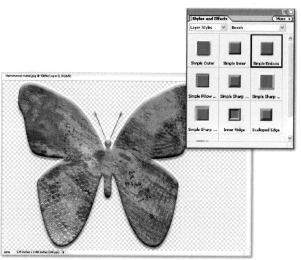

(7) Open the Layer Style dialog box by double-clicking the Layer Style icon on the layer opening the Styles dialog box. Change the Lighting Angle to 90°, Bevel size 20 px, and Bevel Direction to Up.

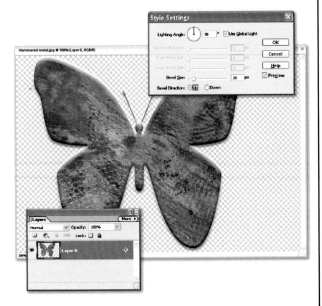

(8) The problem with using the Layer Style is that, because it is applied to the entire layer, some of its effects go beyond the original shape. Here is how to trim the excess Layer style off of the shape. Flatten the layer (Layer⇨Flatten Image). Load the Selection (Select⇨Load Selection) that was created in step 4, copy its contents to a layer (Ctrl+J), and hide the background in the Layers palette.

(9) Duplicate the layer you just created and label it **Top**. With the Top layer selected, hold down the Alt+Shift keys while dragging one of the corner handles toward the center until the layer is approximately the size shown.

(10) Press the keyboard's arrow keys on to nudge the Top layer up until the antennas of both layers align.

11 Open the Hue Saturation dialog (Ctrl+U) and adjust the Hue to -8, which makes the color of the Top layer slightly more red.

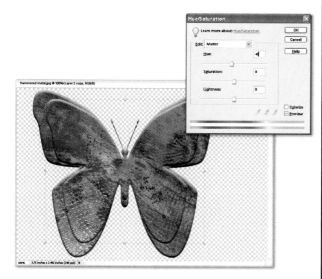

12 Select the Eraser tool and using an Opacity of 20% remove the edges of the Top layer until it appears to blend into the bottom layer as shown.

13 Apply the Plastic Wrap filter (Filter⇨Artistic⇨ Plastic Wrap) and set Highlight Strength to 8, Detail to 5, and Smoothness to 9. The butterfly is finished.

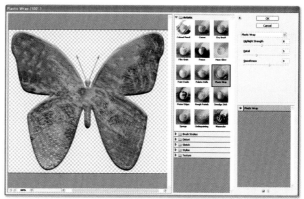

14 To create a background for the butterfly, open the image Wall.jpg. After opening the image, use the move tool and drag the image on top of the Butterfly image to make it into a layer. In the Layers palette, drag the wall below the butterfly layer. Close the Wall.jpg image and do not save any changes if asked.

15 With the Butterfly layer selected, double-click the Noisy Drop Shadow preset in the Layers and Effect palette.

16 Select the Move tool (V) and reduce the size of the butterfly. Finally, reposition the butterfly as shown.

17 Ensure the Foreground color is white. Select the Horizontal Type tool and the set the Font in the Options bar to 24 pt Stencil Std. Click the image and type **iron butterfly**.

18 From the Layer and Effects palette, select and apply the Sprayed Stencil tool by double-clicking on it. This action completes the task.

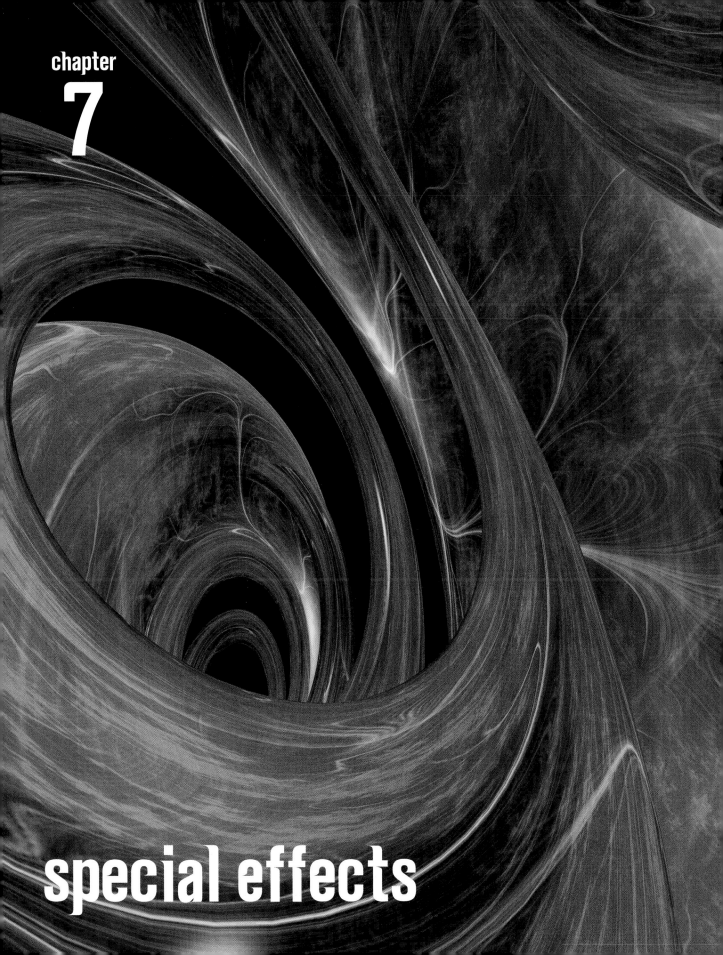

chapter
7

special effects

A classic study of the U.S. Supreme Court cases between 1792 and 1845 and its effect on the homeless moose population in the Middle East

Demystifying the Supreme Court

$24.95

There is hardly a movie made today that doesn't include a budget for special effects, also known as *FX*. Special effects are not new; they have been around for almost as long as people have been making movies. They cover a broad range of visual trickery, from the mansion interiors in *Gone with the Wind* to movies shot entirely in front of a blue screen. Just because you don't make movies doesn't mean you cannot create your own special effects in your photos. In this chapter, I show you how to turn clouds into billowing smoke, create photos that are a cross between Pleasantville and Ansel Adams, create a great paint job for your car, make photos into puzzles and make an American Bald Eagle even more patriotic.

A Walk in the Clouds

Making an individual appear to be in a swirl of smoke or clouds is a cool and easy effect to create. This task uses a layer mask, but the most important part is having a good photo of clouds to work with. To acquire a usuable collection of clouds, make a habit of taking a photo anytime you see good-looking or unusual clouds in the sky. In this task, you will use a photograph of a creature that stands out in front of a store called Creatures of Delight (www.creaturesofdelight.com).

① Open the image Creature.psd. There are several ways in Elements to select the creature and remove the background. One way is to use the Magic Extractor (which is new in Elements 4). Choose Image⇨Magic Extractor and, when the dialog box opens, identify the foreground and the background by painting on the image with the Foreground Brush tool and the Background Brush tool. Because the background is complicated, some trial and error may be required to extract the foreground elements from the background satisfactorily; but this is as good a time as any to practice using the new tool. If you don't want to create a selection, I saved the creature selection that I made in the PSD file, so you can load the selection (Select⇨Load Selection), invert it, and click the Del key to remove the background.

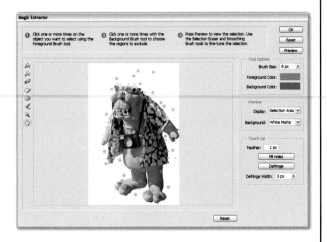

② Open the clouds.psd file, which is a photo of a cloud mass rolling into Florida. Apply Auto Contrast to the clouds to give them some extra impact. Drag the creature over on top of the clouds image.

TIP

When working with a photo of clouds with no blue sky showing, you should experiment with applying Auto Contrast to improve the appearance by bringing out detail in the clouds that would otherwise be lost. The reason Auto Contrast is not a good candidate for a blue sky and clouds photo is its tendency to shift the blue sky to a dark, almost black, shade of blue.

3 Next, you need to add a layer mask. Because Elements doesn't have a layer mask, we need to make one. Select the Background and add a Levels adjustment level (choose Layer⇨New Adjustment Layer⇨Levels). When asked, change the name to **Layer Mask.**

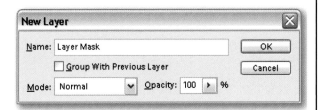

4 When the Levels dialog box appears, don't make any changes; just click OK. Select the top layer and group it with our Layer Mask (Ctrl+G).

5 This is the fun part. In the Layers palette, select the Layer Mask thumbnail. Choose the Brush tool and paint black anywhere on the image that you want the creature to be invisible. The darker the black, the more invisible the top layer is, which gives the appearance that the clouds are in front of the creature.

TIP

Working with a layer mask is a lot easier using a pressure sensitive stylus. I recommend changing the Tablet options so pressure setting of the stylus controls the opacity of the Brush.

To see the layer mask, hold down the Alt key and click on the layer mask thumbnail in the Layers palette.

6 Although you can put the clouds anywhere, you still want the viewer to see the subject; after all, the subject is coming out of the clouds. You will achieve the best effect by using a soft brush at a low Opacity setting to create semitransparent wisps of clouds over the subject, like the ones shown in the final image.

Isolated Color

Long before the movie *Pleasantville* appeared on the screen, removing the color (desaturating) from everything but the subject was a popular way to draw attention to that subject. The best part about this task is that it is too simple to believe, and the only hard part about it is deciding what parts to keep color and what parts to desaturate.

1 Open the file road.psd and create a Hue/Saturation adjustment layer (Layer⇨New Adjustment Layer⇨Hue/Saturation). Click OK to keep the default name. When the Hue/Saturation dialog box appears, drag the Saturation slider all the way to the left and click OK. The photo appears to have lost all color. The photo still contains all of the color, but the color doesn't display because it is filtered through the adjustment layer.

2 Select the Brush tool and make the color black. In the Layers palette, select the Adjustment Layer Mask thumbnail by clicking on it.

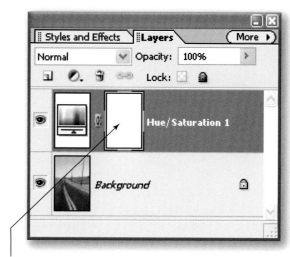

Adjustment Layer Mask thumbnail

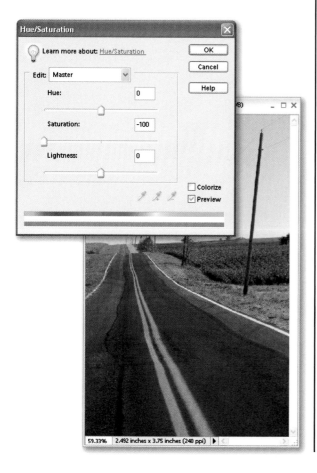

3 With the cursor on the photo, begin to paint on the road to restore the road with its yellow stripe as shown in the Background layer. Wherever you paint with the brush, the desaturation is removed. Even though the road is black, and the color loss isn't apparent you should paint over the entire road. If you accidentally paint outside the road, just paint over the area with white paint. You can see what the layer mask looks like at any time by holding down the Alt key and clicking the thumbnail in the Layers palette; you can toggle back the same way. Why would you want to do this? It is a great way to see what areas in a mask you may have missed.

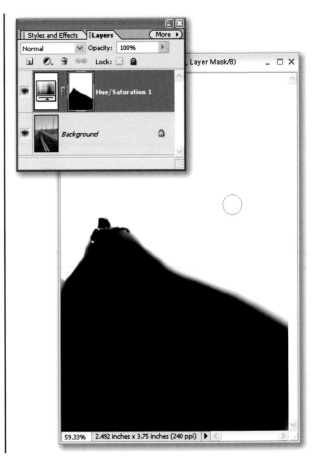

TIP

You can quickly change between foreground and background colors by clicking the X key.

4 That's all there is to it. The resulting image looks like Ansel Adams hits the road — with a yellow stripe.

Patriotic Eagle

Superimposing one image over another was an effect I discovered the first time I accidentally double-exposed a frame of film in my camera. Back in those days you had to manually advance the film after each shot. I loved the effect and used to do a lot of double exposures. Although some digital cameras offer a double-exposure mode, it is much easier to take two separate photos and then combine them in Adobe Photoshop Elements. In this project, you use the layer mask technique that's used throughout the chapter and introduce the Displacement plug-in filter.

① Open eagle.psd, duplicate the image (File⇨Duplicate), and name it **Layer mask insert**. Remove all of the color from the duplicate (Shift+Ctrl+U).

Photo courtesy of istockphoto.com

② Select the entire image in Layer mask insert (Ctrl+A) and copy it to the Clipboard. Minimize the image, as we will need it later. Return to eagle.psd and add a Levels adjustment layer (Layer⇨New Adjustment Layer⇨Levels). Name it Layer Mask, click OK and OK again.

③ Alt-Click on the Layer Mask thumbnail in the Layers palette. The blank layer mask replaces the image of the eagle in the image window.

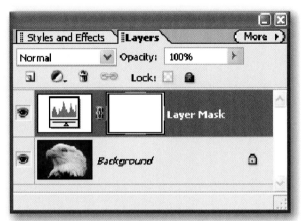

④ Paste the eagle from the Clipboard into the window. Deselect what's selected (Ctrl+D), and then Alt-click the image. This returns the original eagle to the image window and the grayscale eagle is now in the Layer Mask layer. Phew.

(5) Open flag.psd, which is a photo taken of the United States flag on a windy day, cropped for use with this task. Select the Move tool and drag the image from flag.psd to eagle.psd. Close flag.psd. Select the flag layer in the Layers palette and group it with the Layer Mask adjustment layer (Ctrl+G).

(6) With the Flag layer still selected, use the Move tool (V) to drag the flag layer down and to the right as shown.

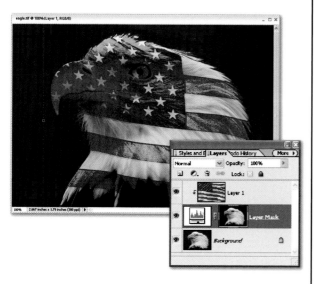

(7) The lines on the flag are smooth and even, but you want them to appear to be part of the eagle's feathers. So save the Layer Mask image that you minimized earlier as **Layer mask insert.psd**. It is very important that it be saved as a PSD file. It's also important that it either be flattened, or saved with maximum compatibility (if you only have an unflattened image with layers, it won't work). Remember where you saved it. Open the Displace filter (Filter⇨Distort⇨Displace). Change the settings to match those shown.

(8) When asked, load Layer mask insert.psd as the displacement map. The filter will displace pixels in the flag by an amount determined by the grayscale reading of the corresponding pixel in the mask. Clicking OK distorts the flag so that it now appears to be part of the eagle's feathers.

9 Change the blend mode to Linear Light.

10 For the final cleanup, select the Layer Mask thumbnail and, using the Brush tool and the colors black and white, remove and add parts of the flag by making areas of the mask lighter or darker. Pay special attention to the eye and the beak. You want the eye to be clear, meaning that all of the area on the mask should be black. On the beak, you want to preserve the stars.

New Paint Job for Cars

Growing up in Los Angeles, I was raised on TV commercials telling viewers that they could get their cars repainted for $29.95. With Elements, replacing the paint job or pattern on a car or any other object isn't all that complicated, and it's free. Ironically, just as with a real paint job, the difference between a good job and a poor one is in the preparation. With a real car, the key is the taping of all of the tiny areas that should not be painted, whereas with this Elements technique it is the creation of an accurate selection. Even with all of the new auto selection tools in Elements, making a good selection takes time. I spent at least 30 minutes creating the one for this car, and I have included the selection in the file Antique car.psd. In this task, I demonstrate several different ways to change the paint color or add a pattern.

(1) Open Antique car.psd and load the selection (Select⊃Load Selection) named Outline. I recommend turning off the "marching ants" marquee (Ctrl+H).

(2) In the Layers palette, add a new layer. Change the foreground color to blue and use the Paint Bucket tool (K) to click on the car inside the selection. Wow! Pretty ugly, right?

(3) Change the blend mode of the layer to Linear Light. This doesn't look very realistic, so lower the Opacity of the layer to 60%. You can use a lot of different blend modes. Most of the ...light Blending modes Linear Light, Soft Light, and so on can be used for different shades of effects.

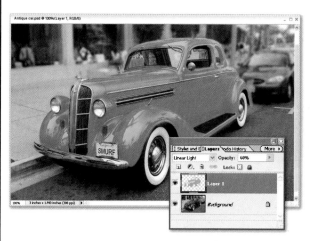

(4) Finally, try the Color blend mode at 70%.

⑤ Let's remove the top layer and replace it with a new one. In this step, we are going to fill the layer with a pattern. Open Fill Layer and select Pattern for Contents. From the default pattern list, pick Optical Checkerboard.

NOTE

I didn't have you use Undo, as Elements records every change of the blend mode as an Undo step; if you were experimenting with different blend modes (good for you), it would take a lot of Undo steps to get back to an empty layer.

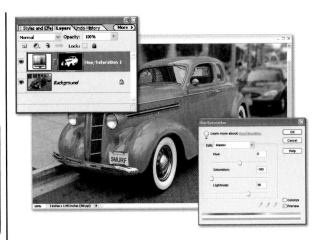

⑥ Click OK to apply the pattern to the top layer. Change the blend mode of the layer to Overlay.

⑦ Elements artists can also use photographs as patterns. Delete the top layer. Because the original colors are so dark, you must lighten them and make them neutral. To do this, create a Hue/Saturation Adjustment layer. Keep the default name but change the Hue/Saturation settings at Hue 0, Saturation 100, and Lightness 30. Click OK and the car is now a medium dark gray. In the Layers palette, notice that the original selection was read by Elements and now appears in the Layer Mask thumbnail.

⑧ Open clouds.psd from the Web site. Choose Edit⇨Define Pattern. Accept the default name that appears. In the Layers palette, add a new layer and group it (Ctrl+G) to the adjustment layer. Choose Edit⇨Fill Layer and choose the clouds.psd pattern. All of the reflections are shaded areas on the car are used by the Blending modes to modify the cloud photograph. This creates the appearance that the photograph is actually following the curves of the vehicle, when in fact it is not.

9 The last variation of the image is finished, but in truth there is much more that you can do, such as applying gradient fills or photos of your kids. The possibilities are endless.

A Monumental Task

Mark Twain once said, "Society honors its live conformists and its dead nonconformists." This honor typically comes in the form of a memorial, a statue, or, in modern times, having something (usually a street or an airport) named after the honoree. With all of the capabilites present in Photoshop Elements, it seems appropriate to use those tools to create appropriate monuments for some of the great leaders of our time. In ancient times, when a new ediface was being built, the most handy source of building materials was obtained by dismantling and using previous monuments. See, recycling isn't all that new of a concept. In this project, you use parts of several monuments found in the U.S. and combine them to create a memorial to a true leader of the people. There were several reasons to choose Sam the Eagle, but the most compelling was that I happen to have a bust of Sam the Eagle on my desk. Before you start the project, you need to download the files Stone eagle.psd, Sam Eagle.psd, and steps and pillars.psd from www.wiley.com/go/elementsgonewild.

① Open the photo Stone eagle.psd. This is the original photo that was a building ornament in Washington DC. You can use the Magnetic Lasso tool to create a selection around the eagle as shown or use the selection I made and load the (Select➪Load Selection) using the selection named *eagle*.

② Convert the selection to a layer (Ctrl+J) and name the layer Eagle 1. Hide the background by clicking the eye of the background in the Layers palette.

③ Open the image Steps and pillars.psd and using the Move (V) tool drag a copy of the eagle from the first photo onto this one.

④ Drag another copy of the eagle and put it as shown. With the second eagle still selected, flip it horizontally (Image⇨Rotate⇨Flip layer horizontal) and use the arrow keys to nudge it next to the first eagle.

⑤ Open the image Sam Eagle.psd. Sam appears in this natural color (blue, white, and blue) but for a marble edifice, you must change the colors so that they are closer to that of his marbled cousins. Open Hue/Saturation (Ctrl+U) and in the dialog box, check the Colorize box, change the settings to Hue: 63°, Saturation: 14, and Lightness: −3.

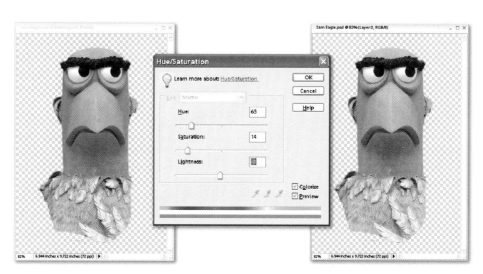

6 Drag a copy of Sam the Eagle onto the Steps and Pillars photo and close it without saving any changes. With the Move tool, position the head as shown next. Select the Eraser tool and choose a brush size of around 20 pixels (px) and set the Opacity to 50%. Erase the bottom edge of Sam's feathers so that it blends in with the other eagles as shown.

7 Sam still has too much color in the bottom feathers, so select the Sponge tool from the Tools palette and using a setting of 80%, desaturate the lower feathers more so that they blend into the others as much as possible. Also apply the Eraser again at a low setting (20% Opacity) along the vertical edges to also improve the blending as shown. Change Sam's Layer opacity to 90%.

8 Now you need to do one last thing to make Sam look like he is made of hard material. With Sam still selected, click the Lock Transparent pixels icon. Choose the Guassian noise (Filter⇨Noise⇨Add Noise) and in the dialog box, select Amount: 3, Distribution: Gaussian, and check the Monochromatic box.

9 In the Layers palette, select all three eagle layers, right-click them, and choose Merge Layers to make them into a single layer. With the layer still selected, hold down the Shift and Alt key while dragging a corner toward the middle to make the eagles smaller. Reduce the size as shown. Double-click on the eagles to apply the size transformation.

10 Ctrl-click the layer thumbnail, creating a selection around the birds. Copy the layer into the clipboard (Ctrl+C). Make the layer invisible by clicking on the eye and remove the selection (Ctrl+D),

11 In the Layers palette, select the background. Load the selection *entrance* and paste the eagles in the clipboard into the selection. (Shit+Ctrl+V). Use to Move tool to reposition the eagles as shown.

12 Load the *entrance* selection again. Choose Filter⇨ Adjustments⇨Photo Filter). In the Photo Filter dialog box, change the settings to Filter: Warming Filter (81), Density: 30%, and uncheck Preserve Luminosity.

13 Remove the entrance selection and you are done.

Producing Puzzling Effects

Puzzle pieces are a great visual clue of something being either mysterious or missing. In earlier days of Photoshop, it was necessary to make your own puzzle pieces, which took too much time and patience for many users. Even though with Elements we have everything we need to create a puzzle built into the application, creating a jigsaw puzzle with Elements is still no piece of cake. You must create and align all of the shapes—some of which don't fit.

---

(1) Create a new 800-x-600-pixel RGB image. Turn on the Grid in the View menu. Select the Custom Shape tool, and from the options bar choose the Shapes drop-down list. I recommend opening the fly-out menu and choosing Large Thumbnail and Objects from the list. This way, each time you open the list, the shapes you need are easy to see.

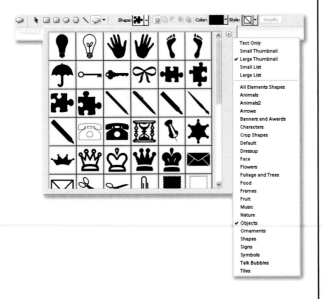

(2) Select the shape Puzzle 3 and drag the shape. The puzzle pieces need to maintain their correct aspect ratio, so, after (not before) you drag the shape, hold down the Constrain (Shift) key. From the Layers palette, select the shape, right-click simplify the shape.

(3) Like a real puzzle, it isn't easy to find pieces that fit. With the first piece in place, select shape Puzzle 2 and drag the puzzle shape until it is the correct size.

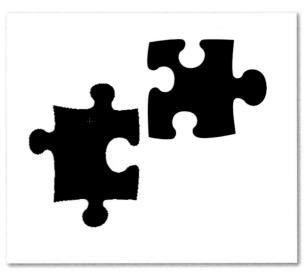

TIP

It is important that you don't hold down the Shift key until after you have started dragging the shape. If you hold down the Shift key before you click the mouse button, Elements puts the shape on the same layer as the previous one — which we do not want to do.

(4) Flip the shape horizontally, and use the Move tool to join it with the previous shape as shown. When you have it in position and the correct size, press the Enter key to apply the transformation.

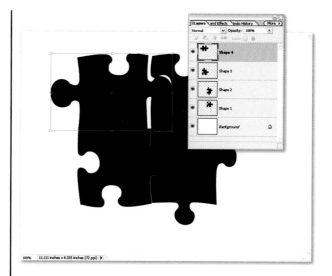

5 Use puzzle 4 and repeat Step 3 as shown.

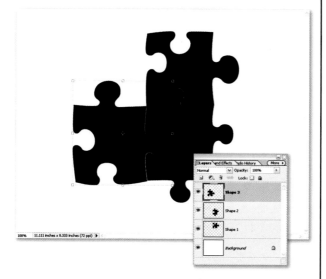

6 Unlike real puzzles, these shape pieces don't fit snuggly. In fact, I don't believe that they were ever made to fit together. For the last shape use Puzzle 1. It won't fit, but after you flip it vertically, you can transform its shape so that it is close to the one shown. Don't forget to apply the transformation by double-clicking or pressing the Enter key and simplifying the layer in the Layers palette. When moving the puzzle piece to get it closer to the others, use the arrow keys rather than the mouse.

7 Open Court.jpg (the U.S. Supreme Court) and drag it to the image we have been working on. Close Court.jpg and don't save any changes if asked. Change the Opacity level of the Court layer to 50% so you can see the puzzle pieces underneath. Reshape the top puzzle layer so that it fits the puzzle pieces as shown. Don't worry about aspect ratios; just make the puzzle piece look like the one shown. Return the Opacity back to 100%.

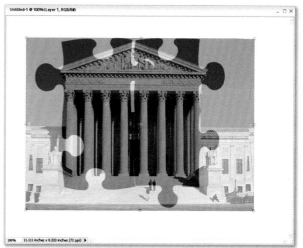

8 In the Layers palette, select the layer containing the photo of the courthouse. While holding down the Ctrl key, click the cursor on the thumbnail of the top puzzle shape (Shape 4), creating a selection of the puzzle shape. With the courthouse layer still selected, press Ctrl+J and a new layer appears that is the part of the photo in the selection.

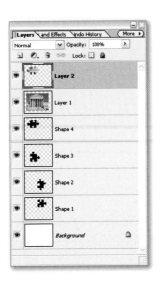

9 Repeat this for each of the other three puzzle shapes. When you are finished, your Layers palette should be very full. Hide the shape layers and the photo layer, and what remains on the screen should be like the one shown below. If everything looks right, you can delete the shape layers and the photo layer in the Layers palette.

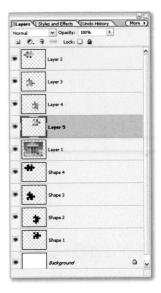

10 Apply the Bevels layer style Simple Sharp Inner to each of the four puzzle pieces, and then apply the Low Drop Shadow layer style.

Rearrange the puzzle pieces with the Move tools. To finish the task, add some text, and use a Simple gradient fill on the Background, and you have an ad for a next bestseller book.

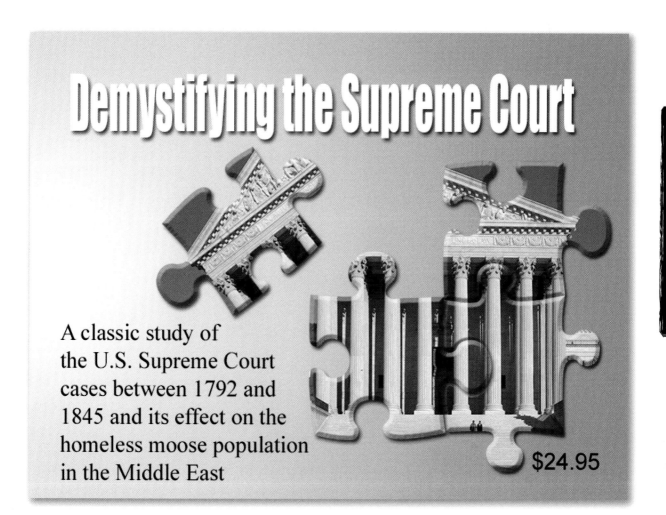

wild text effects

Typefaces have come the full circle. Before Gutenberg, every book had to be copied by hand. The introduction of movable type made it possible to speed up the process without sacrificing quality. Upon seeing a printed book in 1455, Pope Pius II reported it had such neat lettering that one could read it without glasses. Typefaces today have moved from the pursuit of perfection in both shape and form to becoming a medium of communication through their appearance as well as the words they convey. In this section, you explore how to make type into a visual means of communicating the emotion of your message.

The Power of Gold

The single element that is emotionally tied to wealth is gold. Even the humblest object appears to have a lofty purpose if it appears to be made of gold. It's not the most priceless object — pound for pound diamonds are worth far more — but still, when you want to convey the sense of wealth to a viewer, make the subject appear golden. This used to be quite difficult, involving the manipulation of something called *channels* in Photoshop. In Photoshop Elements, making almost any object appear gold plated is quite simple, as with the following simple, eye-catching text effect.

To demonstrate this technique, we are going to make a lobby sign for the most universal bank in the world, known to children everywhere as the Bank of Dad.

(1) We need a fancy wood background to emphasize the gold letters, so create a new 800-x-600-pixel image at a resolution of 72 dpi and with a white Background. Select the Background and then apply the Rosewood texture (Window⇨Style and Effects⇨Wood-Rosewood).

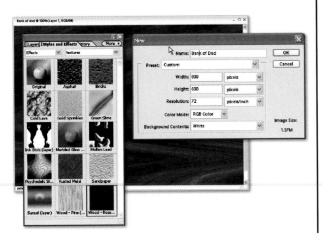

(2) Turn on the Grid (View⇨Grid), and using the Rectangle Marquee Tool drag a selection that is equidistant from the edge of the image as shown. When the selection is in place, turn off the grid.

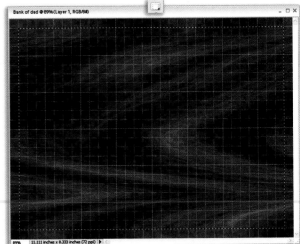

3 Make a layer from the Background (Ctrl+J). Select the Bevels layer style and double click Simple Sharp Pillow Emboss. Flatten the image (Layer⇨Flatten Image). That completes the background.

TIP

Many of the settings in Styles and Effects have long names, so that when in thumbnail view the full names are cut off. To see the names, click the More button in the palette and change from Thumbnail View (default) to the List view.

4 Select the Horizontal Type tool. Because this is a bank that has been around since time began, choose a dignified typeface. The one in the example is Rockwell Extra Bold at 160 points (pt) with the leading set to 130 pt rather than Automatic as shown. Select the word *of* and change it to Rockwell Condensed. Use the Move tool to center the type as shown.

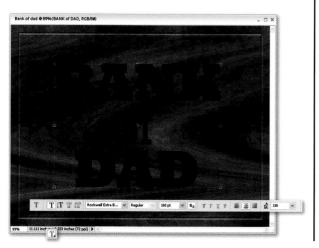

5 Right-click the Type layer, rasterize the type, and then click the Lock button to lock the type layer. Change the foreground color RGB (250, 230, 35). Fill the type with the foreground color (Alt+Backspace).

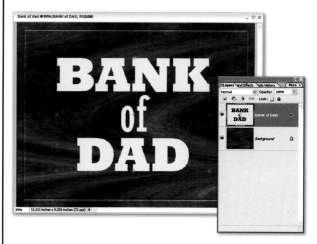

6 Duplicate the type layer by dragging the layer onto the New Layer icon at the top of the Layers palette. Open the Styles and Effects palette, choose Layer Styles, and then click on the Wow-Chrome Reflecting preset to apply it, creating a bright chrome look.

7 To make the text look like gold, change the blending mode to Color burn. Now, select the two layers and merge them together. Open the Styles and Effects palette, choose Layer Styles, and then double-click on the Noisy drop shadow preset to apply it.

What Is the Color of Gold?

There are many types and therefore shades of gold. I picked a base color that produced a gold that had a hint of a green tint to it; because I knew the gold would be in front of a reddish background, avoiding a redder base color prevented the gold from appearing too orange. The advantage of using the combination of a base color and a blending mode allows you to tweak the base color to get a gold that is right for your needs. The best way to adjust the color is to select the lower layer and open the Hue/Saturation (Ctrl+U) dialog box. While looking at the two layers in the image through the blending mode, move the Hue slider to the left or right until the color seen in the image is the color you need.

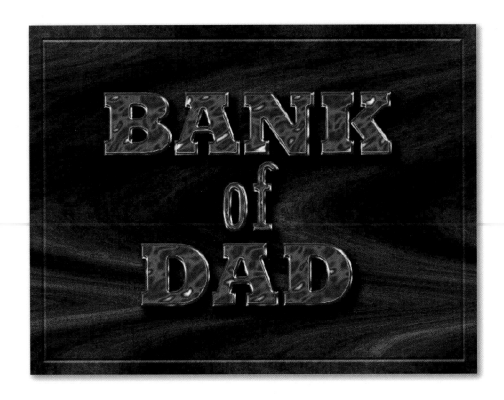

Opposites Attract

By appearance this text effect is a high-contrast attention grabber. It is very easy to do with Photoshop using a Layer Mask, but Photoshop Elements (which doesn't officially have a Layer Mask) requires a workaround to get the same effect. Please note that Photoshop Elements 4 added paragraph text ability, which means that if you're using an earlier version and your text wraps around multiple lines, it will make your image very complex. Because we'll be using the Grid, I recommend that you change the grid settings (Edit, Preferences, Grid) from the default to having a gridline every 100 pixels.

1 Before beginning, change the background color to red. Create a new 400-x-400-pixel image at 72 pixels/inch that uses the background color.

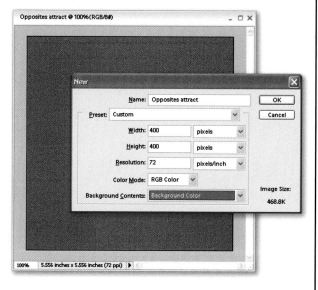

2 Select the Rectangle Marquee tool and drag a selection over half the image as shown. Convert the selection to a layer (Ctrl+J). Change the colors to the defaults (D). In the Layers palette, lock the layer and fill it with the background color (Alt+Backspace). Turn off the grid.

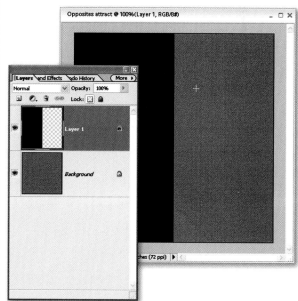

3 Duplicate the shape layer by dragging the layer up to the Create a New Layer icon in the Layers palette and then invert the layer (Ctrl+I), making it a white shape. For the moment, make both the shape layers invisible by clicking on the eye icons.

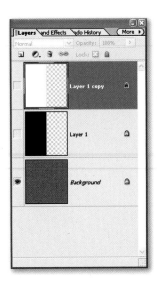

4 Select the Horizontal Type tool and insert your text. The text shown in the example is Arial Black at 36 points using Center alignment. After you have finished, the text will be smaller than the image, so use the Move tool (V) to transform the type layer until it fills the image area as shown. When done, double-click the text to apply the transformation.

5 In the Layers Palette, drag the type layer so that it is between the two shape layers. Make both shape layers visible again. You should see only the black text against the red background at this point.

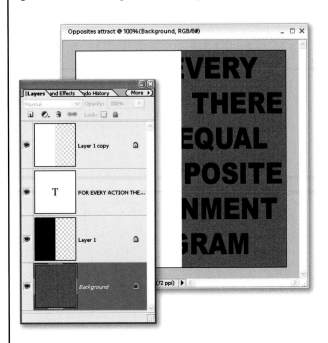

6 Now for the magic part. With the type layer selected, add a Levels adjustment layer (Layers⇨ New Adjustment Layer⇨Levels). When prompted, click OK each time and don't make any changes. With the adjustment layer still selected, group it with the type layer (Ctrl+G). Nothing happens. Now select the top layer and group it (Ctrl+G). All of the text on the left side is filled with white.

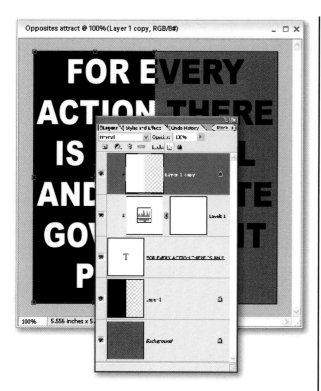

8 After that, you can either keep it as a simple text block or put it in the foreground over a different and larger background as shown below.

7 Here are some variations you can try. Change the foreground color back to red and use the Paint Bucket tool (K) to fill the top white shape with red as shown below. It's all a matter of personal taste.

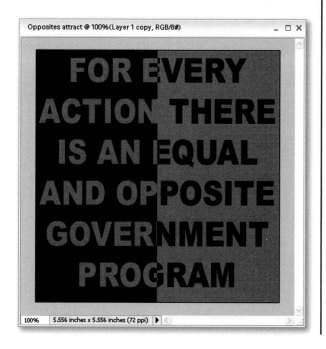

9 With this same technique, you can use one of the predefined shapes to define the reversed area as shown below. The only change in the way I created this variation was that I used a predefined shape (hand) instead of a matching rectangular shape. The background is one of the Styles and Effect Image Effects.

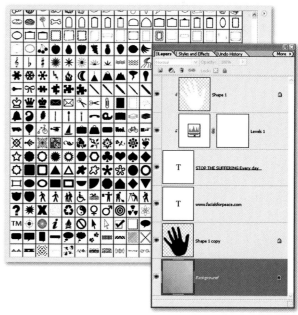

10 The reversal mask layer does not affect the separate line of type containing the fake facialsforpeace.com Web address. To make it reverse like the other text would require either adding the text to the existing type layer (before it is rasterized), or adding separate sets of layer masks. It was much simpler to make sure that the black type didn't disappear into the black hand.

STOP THE SUFFERING
EVERYDAY
THOUSANDS OF CHILDREN ARE IN NEED
OF PROFESSIONAL BEAUTY TREATMENT
WHOSE VILLAGES DO NOT OFFER EVEN
THE MOST BASIC PERSONAL BEAUTY
SERVICES. THESE CHILDREN NEEDLESSLY
SUFFER THE HORROR OF SPLIT ENDS
AND CANNOT EVEN GET A SIMPLE
PEDICURE OR A BIKINI WAX.
BEAUTICIANS WITHOUT BORDERS
IS AN ORGANIZATION OF
PROFESSIONALS WHO VOLUNTEER
THEIR TIME AND BEAUTY PRODUCTS
TO PROVIDE BASIC BEAUTY
TREATMENTS TO CHILDREN AND
ADULTS IN THIRD WORLD COUNTRIES.
www.facialsforpeace.com

Old and Dirty Type

Those of us old enough to remember using typewriters also remember how individual keys could become filled with junk and grime. Dirty keys and worn-out ribbons produced text that looked terrible in the 1950s, but that look is called "grunge" today and is quite popular. This technique is, like others, made up of two parts: First, we need to foul up the type, and then we make an appropriate backdrop.

① Create a new 640-x-480-pixel image that has a white background. If you want to add the text shown, use Lucida Console at a size of 48 points.

CAUTION

If you are using a version of Photoshop Elements earlier than 4.0, you need to add each line separately and then merge them.

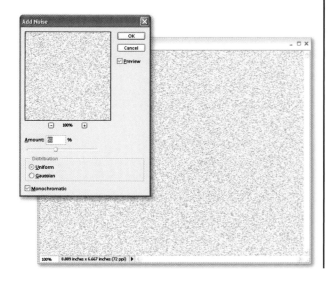

② The type looks clean and crisp, so we need to change that using a custom displacement map. Create another new image the same size as the first and add 50% Uniform noise to it (Monochromatic).

③ From the Filters category in the Styles and Effects palette, select the Color Halftone. Use the default settings shown and apply the halftone. Next, apply a Gaussian Blur at a radius of 1 pixel and save the file as **Grunge Type.psd** in the Displacement maps folder, located in Programs/Adobe/ Photoshop Elements 4.0/Plug-Ins/ Displacement Maps. Yeah, it's really buried down there.

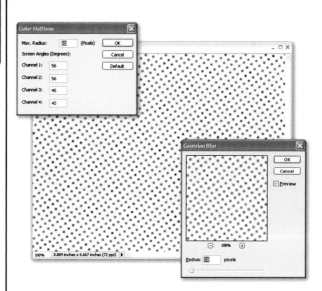

④ Right-click on the Type layer in the Layers palette and rasterize the type. Apply the displacement map that you made in the previous step (Filter⇨Distort⇨ Displace), using the settings shown. Locate the displacement map folder and choose the displacement map.

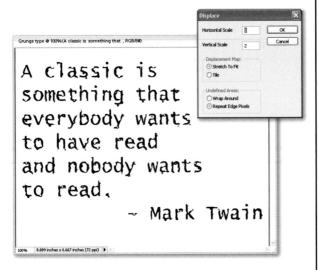

⑤ The dirty type is on a bright white background, so let's tackle that next. In the Layers palette select the Background. Change the foreground color to a tan color as shown and apply it to the Background (Alt+Backspace). This is a little too colorful, but we'll adjust it later.

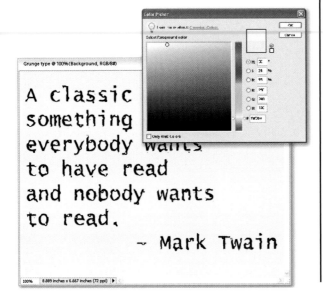

⑥ Now we need to add some texture to the paper. Add a new layer above the Background (Shift+Ctrl+N). Apply a Fill Layer (Edit⇨Fill Layer), select Pattern, and apply the Parchment pattern. What? There's no Parchment pattern on your drop-down menu? That's because Adobe uses a default set of patterns that contains a very small sampling of all of the many patterns that are provided. To see the other pattern sets that are available, click the button on the upper right of the drop-down list. The Parchment pattern is located in the Artist Surfaces category. After applying the pattern, change the blending mode in the Layers palette to Soft Light. It doesn't look like there is much difference; wait, the next layer will bring it all together.

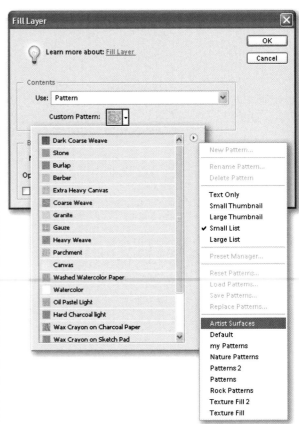

7 Change the colors to the defaults (D) and create a new layer above the pattern layer we just added. Apply the Clouds filter (Filter⇨Render⇨Clouds) and then the Fibers filter using the settings shown. Now apply the Palette Knife filter (Filter⇨Artistic⇨Paint Daubs) using the settings shown.

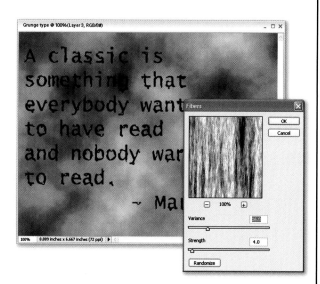

8 Change the opacity of the layer to 75% and then add Gaussian noise at a setting of 5%. To bring it all together, change the blending mode of the layer to Luminosity. Wow.

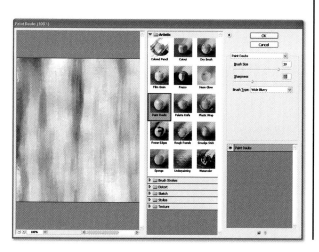

9 The finishing touch is to add some ink splotches and make other minor adjustments. Choose the Custom Shape tool and from the list choose one of the several spatter shapes. Adobe labels these as Crop Shapes; the ones that look like splatters are numbers 33 through 50. After you have applied all of the stains that your heart desires, right-click on the layers and simplify them before merging them together into a single layer. At this point, you may want to reduce the opacity of the stains. In the image shown below, I kept the shapes at 100% opacity and changed the blending mode to Soft Light. Finally, I flattened a copy of the image and applied Auto Contrast.

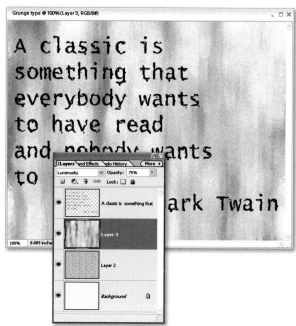

10 There are several possible variations you can create using this technique: by changing the parchment pattern blending mode in Step 6 from Soft Light to Color burn, and by using Palette Knife instead of Paint Daubs in Step 7. You can fiddle with the blending modes and get more of a true grunge appearance as shown.

11 Even without the text, by increasing the intensity of the Artistic filters you can create some awesome backgrounds. In the sample shown, the layer from Step 7 that was done with a Palette Knife filter has been duplicated and placed on top; all three layers use a Color Burn blending mode.

A classic is
something that
everybody wants
to have read
and nobody wants
to read.

~ Mark Twain

Awesome Power Type

There's nothing like some lightning bolts swirling around text or other objects to evoke feelings of raw power. As a Texan who pays high electric bills every summer, seeing electricity zapping all around the place makes my wallet cringe. The creation of the electric field isn't complicated, but it takes quite a few steps. The results are worth all of the effort. We'll start by creating the electric field.

1 Create a new 640-x-480-pixel image that has a transparent Background. Make sure that Elements is set to default colors (D). Apply Clouds to the image (Filter⇨Render⇨Clouds). After doing that, duplicate the layer by dragging the palette layer onto the Create New Layer icon in the Layers palette. Because this technique requires multiple applications of the same filter set, we need to make a total of four clouds layers.

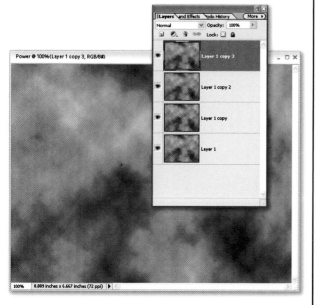

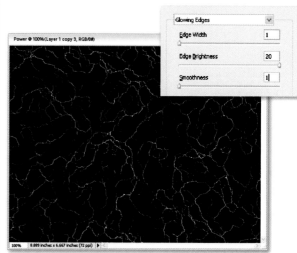

3 Select the layer below the top layer and apply the same filter effects to it (Ctrl+F). Reselect the top layer and change the blending mode to Screen before merging the two layers together.

TIP

The Ctrl+F feature reapplies the last filter used, so if you perform any other actions in the Filter menu, you cannot use Ctrl+F and must repeat the steps in Step 2.

2 In this step we are going to apply two filters to a layer at the same time. Select the top layer and then apply the Palette Knife (Filter⇨Artistic⇨Palette Knife) filter. Change the settings as follows: Stroke Size: 25, Stroke Detail: 3, and Softness: 0. Down at the bottom right of the filter dialog box is an icon called New Effect Layer. Clicking on the icon once makes the Palette Knife the first filter that will be applied. Note that two Palette Knife boxes appear in the box: the lighter one is only indicating that it is currently on the Palette Knife filter. Don't click the OK button. Instead, open the Stylize tab and choose Glowing Edges. Change the settings to an Edge Width: 1, Edge Brightness: 25, and Smoothness: 1. Now click OK.

4 Apply the filters (Ctrl+F) to the remaining untouched cloud layers, first one and then the other. Apply a Gaussian Blur at a radius setting of 3 pixels to the bottom layer. After blurring the layer, open Levels

(Ctrl+L) and push the right slider until it is at the beginning of the slope of the curve. Change the upper blending mode to Screen and then merge these two layers together.

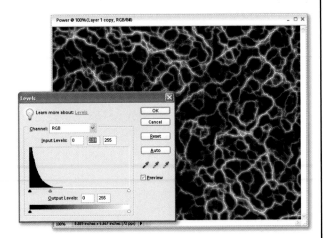

5 Change the blending mode of the top layer to Screen and merge the remaining two layers together. Now we'll add some color by applying Hue/Saturation (Ctrl+U) and checking the Colorize box. Arching electricity tends to be blue, so change the Hue to a value around 200. Increase the Saturation to 60 (a very high value, but this is a special effect.). The resulting electric field is shown next.

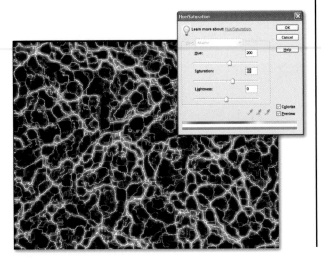

6 There are a lot of things we can do with an electrical storm like this. Because this is the type chapter, let's begin with adding some juice to the type. Create a new 800-x-600-pixel image that has a black Background and drag the layer from the previous image over to the new image. Save and close the electric image as electric.psd so you can always return to it.

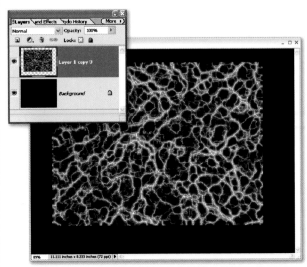

7 Add a Horizontal Type layer and enter the text you want to use. In the example, I used Britannic Bold at 220 pt. Change the foreground color to red and fill the type with it (Ctrl+Backspace).

8 Rasterize the type and then duplicate the layer. To the top type layer apply the Wow-Chrome Reflecting layer style. Change the blending mode to Overlay and then merge both type layers together.

9 Duplicate the electric field layer and open Levels. Move the middle slider to the right until it reads about .27, and then move the right slider to the left until it reads 222. These settings are not exact, but you are trying to make the lines in the top copy thin and bright.

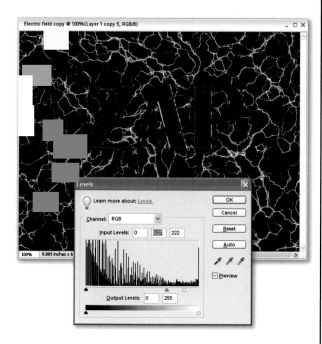

10 Change the blending mode of the top layer to Soft Light. To make the type a little brighter, apply Levels to the type layer. Change the middle setting (gamma) to .60 and the right setting (highlights) to 160. After applying Levels, change the type layer's blending mode to Lighten.

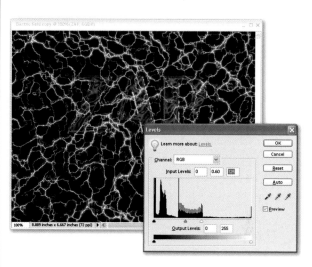

11 You're almost there. Make a new layer and fill it with black. Move it to the bottom of the Layers palette where it will act as the Background. With the black layer selected, add a Level adjustment layer (Layer⇨New Adjustment Layer⇨Levels). Select the Layer Mask thumbnail on the adjustment layer and use the Fill Layer command to fill it with black. Select the electric field above the adjustment layer and group it with the adjustment layer (Ctrl+G). The only thing that should be on the screen now is the red type.

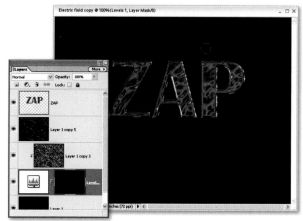

12 Set the colors to their default settings. In the Layers palette, select the adjustment layer mask thumbnail. Select a brush and change the color to white (the X key swaps between foreground and background). Everywhere on the image that you paint white reveals the electric field, and anywhere you paint black makes the electric field invisible. Two variations of this type treatment are shown. In the first I added an extra layer above the black layer and painted a very light blue around the electricity to give the impression of ionization. In the second one, I added a layer and put in a light swash of red paint to give the illusion of the red type reflecting on a polished surface.

Before leaving this lengthy topic, I want to include two other variations that involve using a different color and type treatment. In the first variation I included a blue reflection on the bottom. After finishing this image, I flattened it and applied several Lens Flare filters at various points. Because there are so many blending layers, it is almost impossible to apply a Lens Flare without flattening the image. The second variation shows an example of using black type with an outer glow (so you can see the type) created using an Outer Glow layer style.

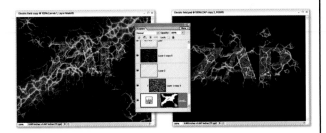

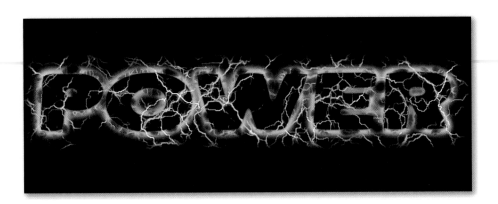

Stone Cold Text

The viewer expects text to look smooth and precise. To give type (and its message) an organic look, this first section shows how to make text appear to be chiseled out of stone. Making images appear to be carved into a material like stone or wood used to require some sophisticated Photoshop magic. With Photoshop Elements, it is a relatively simple procedure. To demonstrate this little wonder, we are going to add a name and epitaph to a headstone. To add to the effect, we will use a photograph of a real headstone. In case you are wondering how I found a black headstone in a cemetery that dates back to the 1830's, the answer is simple: I took a photo of the back of the headstone.

① Open headstone.psd and make a layer from the Background. Turn off the new layer so only the Background is visible and select the Background.

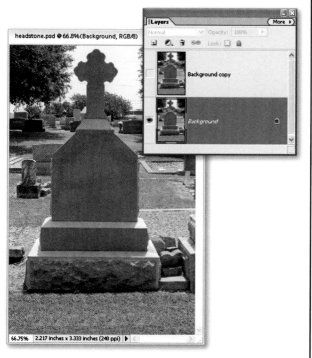

② Use Levels (Ctrl+L) to lighten the Background. Change the middle input value to 2.0 and click OK. Apply noise to the Background (Filter⇨Noise⇨Add Noise). Use a setting of 20%, with Uniform selected and Monochromatic checked. Apply a Gaussian Blur at a radius setting of 2 pixels to smooth out what will be the carved-out area of the text.

3 Make the top layer visible again and select it in the Layers palette. To make working on the image easier, zoom in to 100% (Actual Pixels). Choose the Horizontal Type tool in the Toolbox and change the font to Gill Sans MT at a size of 36 pts. Type the name **ELVIS** and position the type as shown. Highlight the type, choose Warp Text from the options bar, and select Bulge for the Style.

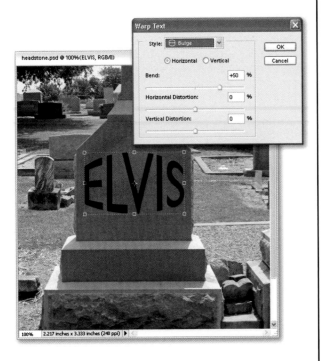

4 Change the type size to 14 points, add the epitaph, and then stretch the type to fit the bottom of the tombstone as shown. When finished, double-click the type to apply the transformation. Select both type layers. Right-click and choose to rasterize the type. Right-click again and choose Merge Layers.

5 Select the Magic Wand tool and, with Contiguous unchecked, click anywhere on the text to select it all. You may want to turn off the marquee (Ctrl+H) to see what happens next. Delete the text layer because we're finished with it. Select the Background copy and click the Delete key. The lighter Background becomes visible.

6 Open the Styles and Effects palette, choose Layer Styles, and then double-click on the Low Drop Shadow preset to apply it to the top layer. The default setting is too large, but we'll fix that in a moment. Select the Bevels layer style and double-click on the Simple Inner preset to apply it. As you can see, the presets are way too large for such a small image, so let's correct that.

7 Because both of the default values are too large, open the Style Settings by double-clicking on the Styles icon in the Layers palette. Change the Shadow Distance to 2 pixels (px) and the Bevel Size to 5 px. Because the bevel was also applied to the edges of the top layer, flatten the image and use the Crop tool to trim off the unwanted edge bevel.

Is It an Inee or an Outee?

When giving the appearance of depth, your own eyes can deceive you. Some may look at the headstone you just made and say that the text doesn't appear so much carved out as raised (embossed). This is a common optical illusion, as both carved and embossed effects appear identical. The viewer unknowingly gets clues from the shadows in the photo, which indicate what direction the light is coming from, and therefore perceives the carved quality of the letters. In this case the sun was coming from the upper right, which is the direction the light-source box in the Drop Shadows layer style indicated, thereby making the shadows correct for a carved appearance.

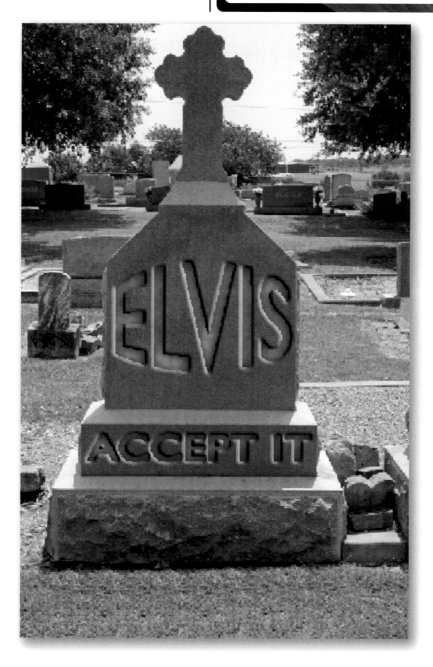

Weathered Copper Text

Carrying the technique we just used a little further, we'll make type that looks made of hammered copper, and that has developed a green patina from being exposed to the outdoors. The base texture used to create the hammered copper comes from a digital photograph I took of a limestone wall.

(1) Open the image stoned.psd. Copy the Background into a layer and make the original Background invisible by clicking the eye icon in the Layers palette.

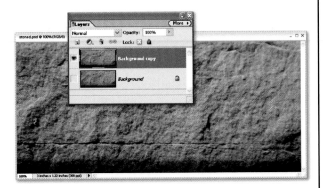

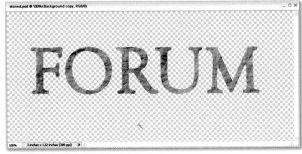

(2) Select the Horizontal Type tool. Using 48-point Goudy Old Style, enter **FORUM**. When finished, use the Move tool to center the text in the image. Using the Magic Wand tool, click inside the text (with Contiguous unselected) and delete the text layer. Invert the selection (Ctrl+Shift+I) and press the Delete key. Get rid of the selection (Ctrl+D).

(3) Select the Bevels layer style and double-click on the Simple Sharp Inner preset to apply it.

4 At this point, you have some nice chiseled stone, but to achieve the appearance of patina-colored copper, we need to use Hue/Saturation (Ctrl+U). With the text layer selected, check Colorize in the dialog box and change the Hue setting to 126 (or whatever setting tickles your fancy).

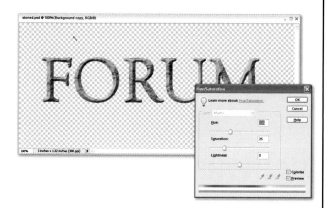

5 Something that sounds as classy as FORUM needs a fancy background. In the Layers palette, make the Background visible again and select it. In the Styles and Effects palette, double-click the Wood-Rosewood setting to create a wood background.

6 At this point, we need a rounded rectangle selection. Because Adobe didn't provide one, we need a workaround. Choose the Shape tool, select the Rounded Rectangle in the options bar, and change the Radius to 30 px. Drag a shape that is equidistant from the edges of the image as shown. I turned on the grid (View⇨Grid) as a guide. Using the Magic Wand tool, click inside the shape. When the message appears telling you the shape layer must be simplified before proceeding, click OK. We're done with the shape, so delete it.

7 Create a new layer from the selection (Ctrl+J). With the new layer selected, choose the Bevels layer style and double-click on the Simple Inner preset to apply it. Select the text and apply a Low drop shadow as shown.

227

8 For the final touch, in the Layers Palette select the wood fill layer above the Background and change the blending mode to Luminosity. The fake copper still appears to be too smooth, so select the layer containing the type, lock the layer, and apply Uniform Noise at a 20% (Monochromatic).

Twisted Text

This is a quick and easy type effect that takes advantage of several of the built-in styles in Photoshop Elements.

1 Open a new 640-x-480-pixel image that has a white Background. Select the Type tool and 120-point Palatino Linotype. Apply Warp Text using the Flag setting.

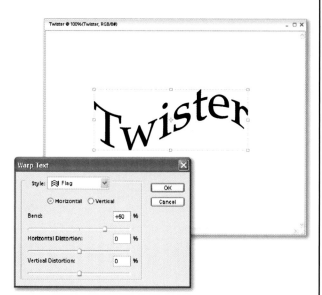

2 Apply one of the Wow Plastic layer styles. Rasterize the type layer and then make a duplicate of it. Select the Move tool (V) and place the cursor outside of the corner handle until it becomes a double-headed cursor. Click and rotate the top layer until the bottom bar of the capital *T* barely touches the top bar of the original letter *T* as shown. After rotating it, double-click the text

to apply the transformation (rotation). Apply a different-colored Wow color Plastic layer style to the rotated type. You can change the color at any time. The Wow Color Plastic layer styles replace the previous layer style when applied. For example, I had all six in place, each one a different color, when I realized that Independence Day was only a week away, so I changed the colors after all six were rotated and in place; it took less than a minute. Repeat this procedure until you have six layers of text.

3 In the Layers palette, select all of the type layers and link them together. Rotate the layers so that they are aligned with the image as shown. To make them really stand out against the background, apply the Hard Edge Drop Shadow layer style.

Rock Star Text

When you are trying to communicate a message to potential viewers that are already visually over-whelmed, you need to use materials in your advertising that reinforces the message. For the text, the typeface selection is critical, as is the materials that fills the selected type. I don't think that a CD titled *Music for a Romantic Evening* would send a mixed message to potential buyers if the title was done in grunge style text with nasty paint splatters covering the background. Conversely, I cannot imagine an ad for a Rolling Stones tour that uses delicate wedding text for the name of the tour. To demonstrate the effect that type fill can make, in this task you make a fictional flyer for the next major Rolling Stones tour. The material you use in the text is the riveted rusted mate-rial that was made in Task 26 (see Chapter 4). Don't worry, you don't have to go back there to make it. You will need to download the photos from www.wiley.com/go/elementsgonewild.

① Create a new image that is 800 x 600 pixels, RGB color and a transparent background. Name the image **Ironman**.

② Open the photo Rusty Iron.jpg. Use the Move (V) tool to drag the image onto Ironman. It will appear as a layer in Ironman. Label the layer **Rivets**. Close Rusty Iron and do not save the changes.

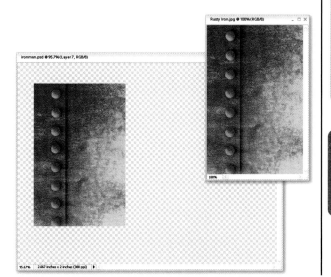

③ Select the Horizontal Type tool from the Tool palette and in the Options bar set the Font to Impact at a size of 120 points (pt) and the color to white. Any light color will work fine. Click on the image and type in a upper case *I*. Use the Move tool to position the first letter as shown.

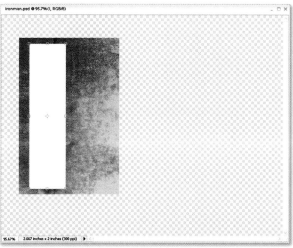

TIP

The image Rusty Iron was created using the technique shown in Task 26.

④ In the Layers palette Ctrl-click the thumbnail of the letter just entered. It will create a selection around the letter. In the Layers palette, delete the letter *I* and select the Rivets layer. The selection from the letter is all that remains over the Rivets layer.

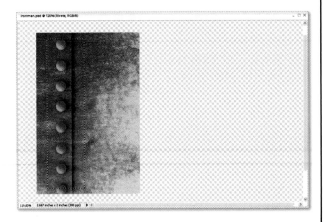

⑤ Copy the selection into a layer (Ctrl+J). In the Layers palette, select the Rivets layer and while holding down the Shift key drag the layer to the right as shown.

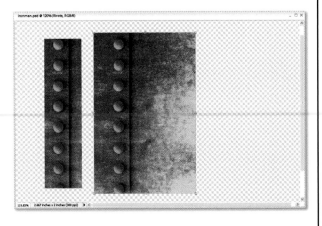

TIP

Holding down the Shift key constrains the movement to only one direction — in this case, the horizontal.

TIP

If Auto Select Layer in the Options bar is checked, you might discover that every time you attempt the drag the Rivets layer, the new letter layer is also being selected and dragged. Just uncheck Auto Select to prevent this or click and drag the very edge of the Rivets layer.

⑥ Select the Horizontal Type tool, click on the image and type an upper case R. Use the Move tool to position it as shown.

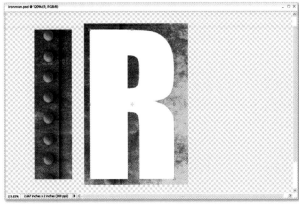

⑦ In the Layers palette Ctrl-click the thumbnail of the letter R and then delete it. Select the Rivets layer and make a layer from the selection (Ctrl+J). Select the Rivets layer again and while holding down the shift key, drag it to the right as shown. The spacing is not critical. If the letters overlap, we correct it later.

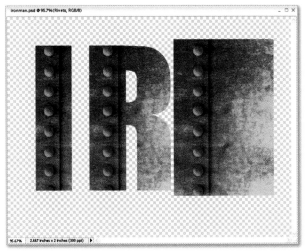

chapter 8 • wild text effects

8 Repeat step 7 twice, once with the letter O and again with the letter N. After you complete the O, you will run out of area for the last letter. Hide the letter O by clicking the Eye icon on its layer and then make the last letter. When you have finished the word IRON, hide the Rivets layer.

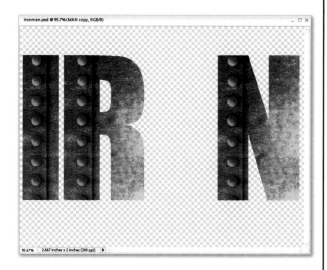

9 To allow the letters to slightly overlap each other in the Layers palette reverse the order of the letters by dragging them one on top of another. Use the Shift Move tool to align the letters as shown.

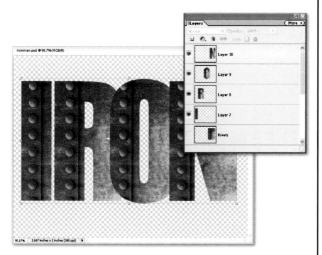

10 Once the letters are in position, select the four letter layers in the Layers palette, right-click on them and choose Merge Layers.

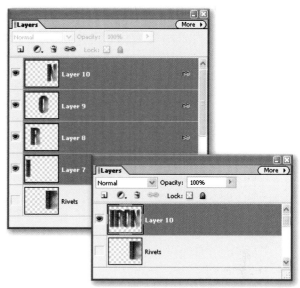

11 Select the merged Iron layer and from the Styles and Effects menu choose the Simple Inner bevel from the Layer Styles menu. The default setting is a little too much so double-click on the layer's Layer Style icon in the Layers Palette and change the Lighting Angle to -90°, the Bezel Size to 8 pixels (px), and the Bevel Direction to Up.

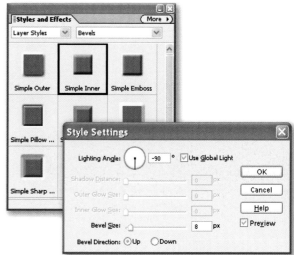

12 In the Layers palette, select the Rivets layer. Open the Style and Effects palette and in the Effects category double click on the Sunset (layer) effect. The background is colorful but it appears to be very polished and smooth. Not the right stuff we need for a rugged Ironman.

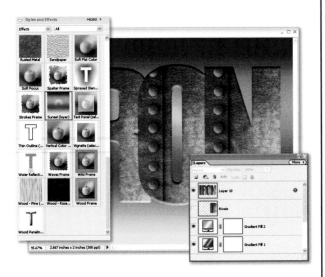

13 In the Layers Palette, select the top Gradient Fill layer (Gradient Fill 2) and click the Create a new layer Icon. A blank layer appears under the text. Change the colors to their default colors (D). Choose Filter⇨Render⇨Clouds. Next, apply Auto Contrast to the layer (Alt+Shift+Ctrl+L) and change the Blend mode to Overlay.

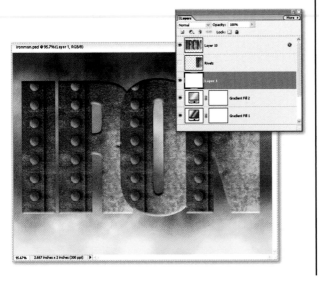

14 To add the word *man*, choose the Horizontal Type tool and change the Font to Stencil with a size of 60 pt. Click anywhere on the image and type **MAN**. From the Styles and Effects palette, double-click on Sprayed Stencil (type). Use the Move tool on the corner of the type to rotate is as shown.

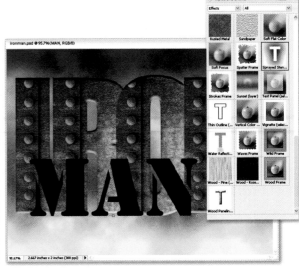

15 It still looks too clean so flatten the image (Layer⇨Flatten). When it asks if it is OK to delete Hidden Layers, say yes. Apply some noise (Filter⇨Noise⇨Add Noise). Change the Amount setting to 8%, set Distribution to Gaussian, and uncheck the Monochromatic box.

16 Final touches now. Choose Canvas Size (Image⇨ Resize⇨Canvas Size). Change the settings in the dialog box to Width: 1, Height: 1, Relative: checked, and Canvas Extension Color: Black. Select the Cookie Cutter tool from the Tools palette, and in the Options drop-down list, choose Crop Shape 22. Click inside the upper-left of the image and drag a shape that nearly touches all of the edges.

17 At this point, you could send this image off to a printer. Or, for something more fun, open the photo brick wall.jpg and drag the Ironman image on top using the Move tool. To allow a little of the bricks in the wall to show through, use the Eraser tool at an Opacity of 15% and lightly thin out some of the areas.

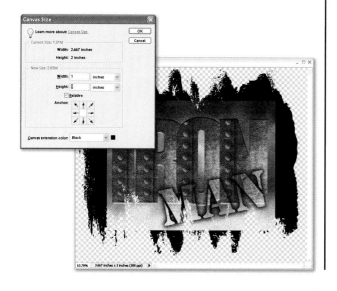

index

3-D shapes. *See* cones example; photos cubed

A

abandoned church.psd file, 99
action figure example
    caveman.psd file, 49
    Clone Stamp tool, 49
    Dodge tool, 49
    flipping, 50
    head.psd file, 49
    Hue/Saturation dialog box, 50
    layers, 50
    Olympic stadium.jpg file, 51
Adjust Color for Skin Tone dialog box, 156
airbrush art example
    highlights, 145
    layers, 145
    Linear Light blending mode, 145
antique car.psd file, paint job for cars example, 193
art
    airbrush example, 145–146
    colored pencil drawing, 147–149
    faded poster print, 150–152
    master image for multiple effects, 133–136
    pencil drawings, 137–140
    people in paintings, 131–132
    still-life conversions, 124–127
    watercolors, 128–130, 141–144

B

Baby and blanket.jpg file, 156
baby photo
    bluebonnet flowers background, 158
    color correction and, 156
    Magic Selection brush, 156
    Rectangular Marquee tool, 158
    sky background, 157
    transformation, 157
background
    baby photo sky background, 157
    blurred, 4
    clouds/smoke example, 184
    color, old-time photo, 95
    eyeball example, 83

    gold plating and, 208
    grunge type, 216
    heavy metal butterfly example, 179
    Opposites Attract, 211
    stone cold text, 223
Bevels layer
    gold plating and, 209
    puzzle pieces, 204
    weathered copper text, 226
Blend mode, windmills example, 116
Blue Checkered Curtain.psd file, glass spheres example, 80
blurring, background, 4
Bob.psd file, TV mockup, 28
bodybuilder example
    Liquify dialog box, 53
    Popeye syndrome, 54
    Warp tool, 54
Brightness/Contrast, TV mockup, 29
Bruce.psd file, pencil drawings, 137
Brush tool
    family resemblance example, 47
    glass spheres example, 82
    isolated color example, 187
    master image and, 134
    postage stamp example, 19
    twisted steel example, 171
Burn tool
    church example, 103
    science fiction scene, 11

C

canvas, size, 75, 90, 107
Canvas tool, science fiction scene, 12
caveman.psd file, action figure example, 49
Chalk & Charcoal filter, pencil drawings and, 137
channels, gold plating and, 208
child.psd file, photos cubed, 62
church example
    abandoned church.psd file, 99
    Burn tool, 103
    Cooling filter, 101
    Eyedropper tool, 105
    foreground color, 102

continued

church example *(continued)*
    Glass filter, 105
    Gradient tool, 100, 103
    layers, 99
    Levels dialog box, 102
    lighting, 99
    Magic Wand tool, 99
    Motion Blur, 101
    Perspective transformation, 104
    Polygonal Lasso tool, 104
    transformation, 104
    Twilight layer, 102
clipping masks, steer horns example, 57
Clone Stamp tool
    action figure example, 49
    family resemblance example, 47
    razor example, 43
    steer horns example, 56
Close Court.jpg, puzzle pieces and, 203
Clouds, old-time photo, 95
Clouds filter
    grunge type, 217
    old-time photo, 97
    rock star text, 234
clouds/smoke example
    background, 184
    Creature.psd file, 184
    foreground, 184
    layer masks, 185
    Magic Extractor, 184
color, isolated. *See* isolated color example
Color Blend mode, wanted poster, 36
Color Burn blend mode
    science fiction scene, 11
    still-life conversions, 126
color correction, baby photo, 156
Color Halftone filter
    comic book example, 14
    grunge type, 215
Color Picker dialog box, 17
colored pencil drawing, 147–149
Colorize option
    old-time photos, 94
    TV mockup, HDTV, 33
comic book example
    Color Halftone filter, 14
    foreground color, 14
    layers, 14
    Minimum filter, 13
    Poster Edges filter, 14
    sad woman.psd file, 13
    Stamp Clone tool, 15

cones example
    Copper fill, 70
    Custom Shape tool, 69
    grid and, 69
    Hue/Saturation option, 71
    layers, 70
    Rectangle custom tool, 70
    Snap to Grid, 69
Cookie Cutter tool
    heavy metal butterfly example, 176–177
    watercolor example II, 143
Cooling filter, church example, 101
Copper fill, cones example, 70
courthouse.psd file, watercolors, 128
Creature.psd file, clouds/smoke example, 184
cropping, TV mockup, 28
Crosshatch filter, pop art example, 17
currency example
    Depth of Field, 26
    Hue/Saturation dialog box, 24
    layers, 25
    smiling face.psd file, 24
    Wave filter, 25
Custom Shape tool
    cones, 69
    grunge type, 217
    old-time photo, 97
    oriental display box, 173
    pop art example, 18
    puzzle pieces, 202
Cutout filter, faded poster print, 150

D

Define Pattern, paint job for cars example, 194
Defringe feature, magazine cover, 5
Depth of Field, currency example, 26
Distort transform tool, photos cubed and, 63
Dodge tool
    action figure example, 49
    earth photo example, 78
    science fiction scene, 11
Duplicate layer dialog box, 10
Duplicate Layer option, 10

E

eagle.psd file, patriotic eagle example, 190
earth photo example
    Dodge tool, 78
    Elliptical Marquee tool, 77

fisheye lens, 77
  Guassian blur and, 78
  layers, 77
  layers, invisible/visible, 78
  Spherize filter, 77
edges, old-time photo, 95
Elliptical Marquee tool
  earth photo example, 77
  eyeball example, 83
  glass spheres example, 80
  twisted steel example, 170, 171
Elliptical Shape tool, eyeball example, 84
Empty glass.jpg file, eyeball example, 86
Eraser tool
  heavy metal butterfly example, 179
  monument example, 198
  twisted steel example, 170
eyeball example
  background, 83
  Elliptical Marquee tool, 83
  Elliptical Shape tool, 84
  Empty glass.jpg file, 86
  Eyedropper tool, 86
  foreground color, 84
  Free Transform tool, 87
  gradients, 83
  grid and, 83
  noise, 84–85
  opacity, 87
  Rectangle Shape tool, 85
  reflection, 85
  Spherize filter, 86
Eyedropper tool
  baby photo, 156
  church example, 105
  eyeball example, 86
  magazine cover, 6
  old-time photo, 96
  science fiction scene, 10

F

faded poster print, 150–152
faking multiple exposure example. *See* multiple exposure example
family resemblance example
  Clone Stamp tool, 47
  Grace.psd file, 45
  opacity, 46
  Tim.tif file, 45

transformation, 46
  transparency, 46
fighter plane.jpg file, flower power example, 113
fills
  layers, paint job for cars example, 194
  pattern fills, 21
  watercolor example II, 143
Find Edges filter, still-life conversions, 124
fire.psd image, science fiction scene, 9
fisheye lens, earth photo example, 77
flatten image, twisted steel example, 169
Flatten image option, watercolors, 142
flipped images
  action figure example, 50
  monument example, 197
  photos cubed and, 63
  twisted steel example, 171
flower power example
  fighter plane.jpg file, 113
  flower.psd file, 111
  Free Transform tool, 112
  layers, 112
  layers, merged, 113
  Lock transparency, 113
  Magnetic Lasso tool, 111
  Move tool, 113
  Styles and Effects palette, 113
flower.psd file, flower power example, 111
flowers.jpg file, baby photo, 158
foreground
  clouds/smoke example, 184
  grunge type, 216
foreground color
  church example, 102
  comic book example, 14
  eyeball example, 84
  heavy metal butterfly example, 180
  old-time photo, 95
frames example
  canvas size, 75
  grids, 73
  layers, 74
  Polygonal Lasso, 74
  Transform tool, 73
  zoom, 74
Free Transform tool
  eyeball example, 87
  flower power example, 112
  multiple exposure example, 108
  pop-up pages, 90
FX, introduction, 183

G

Gallery Effects, 147
gas price.jpg, signs example, 160
Gaussian blur
    earth photo example, 78
    glass spheres example, 81
    grunge type, 215
    Hue/Saturation dialog box, 220
    power type, 219
    TV mockup, 30
Glass Button Layer Style, 33
Glass filter, church example, 105
glass spheres example
    Blue Checkered Curtain.psd file, 80
    Brush tool, 82
    Elliptical Marquee tool, 80
    Gaussian blur, 81
    Inner Glow layer style, 80–81
    layers, 80
    rose.psd file, 80
    Rounded Rectangle tool, 81
    Spherize filter, 81
Glowing Edges filter
    faded poster print, 151
    people in paintings, 131–132
    pop art example, 15
    power type, 219
gold plated text
    background, 208
    Bevels layer, 209
    channels and, 208
    grid and, 208
    Horizontal Type tool, 209
    Rosewood texture, 208
    Simple Sharp Pillow Emboss, 209
    Styles and Effects palette, 210
    Type layer, 209
Grace.psd file, family resemblance example, 45
Gradient Map dialog box, windmills example, 117
Gradient tool, church example, 100, 103
gradients
    eyeball example, 83
    windmills example, 117
Graphic Pen filter, wanted poster, 35
grid
    cones example, 69
    eyeball example, 83
    frames example, 73
    gold plating and, 208
    oriental display box, 174

photos cubed, 62
postage stamp example, 19
puzzle pieces, 202
grunge type
    background, 215, 216
    Clouds filter, 217
    Color Halftone filter, 215
    Custom Shape tool, 217
    foreground, 216
    Gaussian blur, 215
    layers, 216
    noise, 215, 217
    Parchment pattern, 216

H

Hammered metal.jpg file, heavy metal butterfly
  example, 176
Hard Light blending mode, pencil drawings, 140
head.psd file, action figure example, 49
headstone.psd file, stone cold text, 223
heavy metal butterfly example
    background, 179
    Cookie Cutter tool, 176–177
    eraser tool, 179
    Hammered metal.jpg file, 176
    Hue/Saturation dialog box, 179
    layer styles, 178
    Noisy Drop Shadow, 180
    Plastic Wrap filter, 179
    Sprayed Stencil tool, 180
    Styles and Effects palette, 176–177
highlights
    airbrush example, 145
    master image and, 134
Horizontal Type tool
    gold plating, 209
    Opposites Attract, 212
    power type, 220
    rock star text, 231
    titles, 5
    TV mockup, HDTV, 33
    weathered copper text, 226
Hue/Saturation dialog box, 17
    cones, 71
    currency example, 24
    Gaussian blur, 220
    heavy metal butterfly example, 179
    isolated color example, 187
    postage stamp example, 23
    weathered copper text, 227

index

I

Inner Glow layer style, glass spheres example, 80–81
inversion, science fiction scene, 9
isolated color example
    Brush tool, 187
    Hue/Saturation adjustment, 187
    road.psd file, 187
istockphoto.com, 190

L

Lasso tool, selections and, 9
late night church. *See* church example
layer masks
    clouds/smoke example, 185
    Opposites Attract, 211
    patriotic eagle example, 190
    size relationships, 166
layers
    action figure example, 50
    airbrush example, 145
    church example, 99
    comic book example, 14
    cones example, 70
    currency example, 25
    Duplicate Layer option, 10
    duplicating, 6
    earth photo example, 77, 78
    flower power example, 112
    frames example, 74
    Glass Button Layer Style, 33
    glass spheres example, 80
    grunge type, 216
    magazine cover, 8
    masks, 10
    masks, watercolor example, 143
    merge, flower power, 113
    merge, monument example, 199
    multiple exposure example, 107
    new, Opposites Attract and, 212
    old-time photo, 95
    oriental display box, 174
    paint job for cards example, 193
    pop art example, 18
    power type, 219
    puzzle pieces and, 204
    razor example, 40, 41–42
    rock star text, 232
    signs, 161
    still-life conversion, 124
    stone cold text, 224
    styles, heavy metal butterfly example, 178
    TV mockup, 28
    twisted steel example, 169
    windmills example, 116
Layers palette, Duplicate Layer option, 6
layout, magazine cover, 4–8
lightning.psd file, twisted steel example, 171
Linear Light blending mode
    airbrush example, 145
    master image and, 134
    paint job for cars example, 193
    patriotic eagle example, 191
linked layers
    action figure example, 51
    introduction, 51
Liquify dialog box, bodybuilder example, 53
Little brown church.psd file, still-life conversions and, 124
Lock transparency, flower power example, 113
Low Drop Shadow, old-time photo, 97
Luminosity, grunge type, 217

M

magazine cover
    Defringe feature, 5
    Eyedropper tool, 6
    layers, 8
    Magic Wand tool, 4
    Move tool, 4
    realism, 7
    Selection Brush tool, 4
    Shape tool, 7
    Type tool, 7
Magic Extractor
    clouds/smoke example, 184
    multiple exposure example, 107
    pop-up pages, 89
    size relationships and, 165
Magic Selection brush, baby photo, 156
Magic Wand tool
    church example, 99
    magazine layout, 4
    pop-up pages, 90
    postage stamp example, 20
    stone cold text, 224
Magnetic Lasso tool
    flower power example, 111
    monument example, 196
man with glasses.psd, postage stamp example, 21
marching ants marquee, 193

masks
    clipping masks, 57
    layers, 10
master image for multiple effects
    Brush tool and, 134
    highlights, 134
    Linear Light blending mode, 134
    Poster Edges filter, 133
merge layers, flower power example, 113
Minimum filter, comic book example, 13
monster car.psd image, science fiction scene, 9
monument example
    Eraser tool, 198
    flipped, 197
    layer merge, 199
    Magnetic Lasso tool, 196
    noise, 198
    opacity, 198
    Photo filter, 201
    Sam Eagle.psd file, 197
    Sponge tool, 198
    Steps and pillars.psd file, 197
    Stone eagle.psd file, 196
morphing, steer horns example, 56–58
Motion Blur, church example, 101
Move tool
    flower power example, 113
    magazine layout, 4
    multiple exposure example, 108
    patriotic eagle example, 191
    razor example, 40
    signs, 162
    size relationships and, 166
Movie Prime setting, science fiction scene, 12
multiple exposure example
    canvas size, 107
    Free Transform tool, 108
    layers, 107
    Magic Extractor, 107
    Move tool, 108
    rotation, 108
    Skateboard.psd file, 107

N

NASA images, pop-up pages, 89
noise
    eyeball example, 84–85
    grunge type, 215, 217
    monument example, 198
Noisy Drop Shadow, heavy metal butterfly example, 180

O

Oil Medium Brush Wet Edges, watercolor example, 129
Old and Dirty Type. See grunge type
Old building.psd file, old-time photo and, 94
old paper.psd file, wanted poster, 35
old-time photo
    background, 95
    Clouds filter, 97
    Colorize option, 94
    Custom Shape tool, 97
    edges, 95
    Eyedropper tool, 96
    foreground, 95
    layers, 95
    Low Drop Shadow, 97
    Old building photo.psd file, 94
    paper matte, 96
    Ripple filter, 97
    Screen blend mode, 96
    sepia toning, 94
    Spatter filter, 95
    Spray Radius, 95
    Styles and Effects palette, 97
    Texturizer, 96
old truck.psd image, faded poster print, 150
Olympic stadium.jpg file, action figure example, 51
opacity
    eyeball example, 87
    family resemblance example, 46
    monument example, 198
    pencil drawings, 139
Open Court.jpg file, puzzle pieces, 203
Opposites Attract
    background, 211
    Horizontal Type tool, 212
    layer masks, 211
    layers, new, 212
    Paint Bucket tool, 213
    Rectangle Marquee tool, 211
    reversal mask layer, 214
oriental display box
    Custom Shape tool, 173
    grid, 174
    layers, 174
    Paint Bucket tool, 173
    WOW-Chrome Reflecting layer style, 173
Overlay blend mode
    pop art example, 17
    science fiction scene, 11

index

P

Paint Bucket tool
    Opposites Attract, 213
    oriental display box, 173
    pop art example, 17
    postage stamp example, 20
paint job for cars example
    Antique car.psd file, 193
    fill layers, 194
    Linear Light blend mode, 193
painterly effects. *See also* art
    airbrush art, 145–146
    master image for multiple, 133–136
    pencil drawings, 137–140
    people in paintings, 131–132
    still-life conversions, 124–127
    watercolor example, 128–130
    watercolor example II, 141–144
Palette Knife filter, power type, 219
palettes, Style and Effects, 20
paper matte, old-time photo, 96
Parchment pattern, grunge type, 216
patriotic eagle example
    eagle.psd file, 190
    layer mask, 190
    Linear Light blending mode, 191
    Move tool, 191
pencil drawings
    Bruce.psd file, 137
    Chalk & Charcoal filter, 137
    Hard Light blending mode, 139
    opacity, 139
Pencil tool, postage stamp example, 21
people in paintings, 131–132
Perspective transformation, church example, 104
Photo filter, monument example, 201
photos cubed
    child.psd file, 62
    Distort transform tool, 63
    flipping, 63
    grids, 62
    shading, 64
    Skew transformation tool, 62
    variations, 67–68
Plastic Wrap filter, heavy metal butterfly example, 179
Polar Coordinates filter, twisted steel example, 169
Polygonal Lasso tool
    church example, 104
    frames example, 74
    razor example, 40, 42

signs, 162
    size relationships and, 167
pop art example
    Crosshatch filter, 17
    Custom Shape tool, 18
    Glowing Edges filter, 15
    Overlay blend mode, 17
    Paint Bucket tool, 17
    trumpet player.psd, 15
    Watercolor filter, 15
pop-up pages
    canvas size, 90
    Free Transform tool, 90
    Magic Extractor, 89
    Magic Wand tool, 90
    NASA images and, 89
    Shuttle launch.psd file, 89
Popeye syndrome, bodybuilder example, 54
postage stamp example
    fonts, 22
    grid settings, 19
    Magic Wand tool, 20
    Paint Bucket tool, 20
    pattern fills, 21
    Pencil tool, 21
    ruler settings, 19
    Style and Effects palette, 20
Poster Edges filter
    comic book example, 14
    master image, 133
power type
    color, 219
    Gaussian blur, 219
    Glowing Edges filter, 219
    Horizontal Type tool, 220
    layers, 219
    Palette Knife filter, 219
    Soft Light blending mode, 221
    WOW-Chrome Reflecting layer style, 221
puzzle pieces
    Bevels layer, 204
    Close Court.jpg file, 203
    Custom Shape tool, 202
    grid, 202
    layers, 204
    Open Court.jpg file, 203
    Shapes drop-down list, 202

R

Radial Blur, twisted steel example, 170
ramily resemblance example, Brush tool, 47

Rasterize option, TV mockup, 31
razor example
    Clone Stamp tool, 43
    layers, 40, 41–42
    Move tool, 40
    Polygonal Lasso tool, 40, 42
    razor.psd file, 40
    transformation, 42
razor.psd file, razor example, 40
realism, magazine cover, 7
Rectangle custom tool, cones, 70
Rectangle Marquee tool, Opposites Attract, 211
Rectangle shape tool, eyeball example, 85
Rectangular Marquee tool
    baby photo, 158
    twisted steel example, 169
reflection, eyeball example, 85
reversal mask layer, Opposites Attract, 214
Ripple filter, old-time photo, 97
road.psd file, isolated color example, 187
rock star text
    Clouds filter, 234
    Horizontal Type tool, 231
    layers, 232
    Rusty Iron.jpg, 231
    Styles and Effects palette, 233–234
Rose.psd file, glass spheres example, 80
Rosewood texture, gold plating and, 208
rotation
    multiple exposure example, 108
    twisted steel example, 171
Rounded Rectangle tool
    glass spheres example, 81
    TV mockup, 31
ruler, postage stamp example, 19
Rusty Iron.jpg, rock star text, 231

S

sad woman.psd file, 13
Sam Eagle.psd file, monument example, 197
scan lines, TV mockup, 28
science fiction scene
    Burn tool, 11
    Canvas tool, 12
    Clone Stamp tool, 11
    color burn blend mode, 11
    Dodge tool, 11
    Eyedropper tool, 10
    fire.psd image, 9
    inversion, 9
    monster car.psd image, 9

Movie Prime setting, 12
    Overlay blend mode, 11
Screen blend mode, old-time photo, 96
Selection Brush tool, magazine layout, 4
selections
    creation, 9
    Lasso tool, 9
sepia photos. See old-time photo
shading, photos cubed and, 64
Shape tool
    magazine cover, 7
    weathered copper text, 227
Shapes drop-down list, puzzle pieces, 202
Shuttle launch.psd file, pop-up pages, 89
signs
    gas price.jpg, 160
    layers, 161
    Move tool, 162
    Polygonal Lasso tool, 162
    text, 160
    transformation, 161
Simple Sharp Pillow Emboss, gold plating and, 209
size relationships
    layer masks, 166
    Levels dialog box, 166
    Magic Extractor, 165
    Move tool, 166
    Polygonal Lasso tool, 167
    Young woman standing.psd file, 165
Skateboard.psd file, multiple exposure example, 107
Skew transformation tool, photos cubed, 62
Sky.jpg file, baby photo and, 157
smiling face.psd file, currency example, 24
smiling man.psd file, wanted poster, 35
Snap to Grid, cones example, 69
soft edge drop shadow, 20
Soft Light blending mode, power type, 221
Spatter filter, old-time photo, 95
special effects. See FX
spheres, glass. See glass spheres example
Spherize filter
    earth photo example, 77
    eyeball example, 86
    glass spheres example, 81
Sponge tool, monument example, 198
Spray Radius, old-time photo, 95
Sprayed Stencil tool, heavy metal butterfly example, 180
Stamp Clone tool, comic book example, 15
stamp example. See postage stamp example
steer horns example
    clipping masks, 57
    Clone Stamp tool, 56

Steps and pillars.psd file, monument example, 197
still-life conversions. *See also* art
    canvas size, 127
    Color Burn blend mode, 126
    Find Edges filter, 124
    layers, 124
    Little brown church.psd file, 124
stone cold text
    background, 223
    headstone.psd file, 223
    layers, 224
    Magic Wand tool, 224
    Styles and Effects palette, 225
Stone eagle.psd file, monument example, 196
stone.psd file, weathered copper text, 226
Stroke Pressure slider, Chalk & Charcoal filter, 137
Style Settings adjustment box, 97
Styles and Effects palette
    flower power example, 113
    gold plating and, 210
    heavy metal butterfly example, 176–177
    old-time photo, 97
    postage stamp example, 20
    rock star text, 233–234
    stone cold text, 225
    windmills example, 119

T

text
    gold plated, 208–210
    grunge type, 215–218
    opposites, 211–214
    power type, 219–222
    rock star, 231–235
    signs, 160
    stone cold text, 223–225
    twisted, 229–230
    weathered copper, 226–228
Texturizer
    old-time photo, 96
    watercolor example II, 143
Tim.tif file, family resemblance example, 45
Transform tool, frames example, 73
transformation
    baby photo, 157
    church example, 104
    Distort transform tool, 63
    family resemblance example, 46
    razor example, 42
    signs, 161
    Skew tool, 62

transparency
    family resemblance example, 46
    flower power example, 113
trompe l'oeil, 61
trumpet player.psd. *See* pop art example
TV mockup
    Bob.psd file, 28
    Brightness/Contrast, 29
    cropping, 28
    fonts, 30
    Gaussian blur, 30
    HDTV, Colorize option, 33
    layers, 28
    pattern fills, 29
    rasterization, 31
    Rounded Rectangle tool, 31
    scan lines, 28
tweening, steer horns example, 56–58
Twilight layer, church example, 102
twisted steel example
    Brush tool, 171
    Elliptical Marquee tool, 170
    Eraser tool, 170
    flatten image, 169
    flipping, 171
    Flywheel.jpg and, 169
    layers, 169
    lightning.psd file, 171
    Polar Coordinates filter, 169
    Radial Blur, 170
    rotation, 171
    WOW-Plastic Clear layer style, 171
twisted text, 229–230
Type layer, gold plating and, 209
Type tool
    magazine cover, 7
    windmills example, 118

W

wanted poster
    Color Blend mode, 36
    Graphic Pen filter, 35
    old paper.psd file, 35
    smiling man.psd file, 35
Warp tool, bodybuilder example, 54
warped text, windmills example, 118
watercolor example
    courthouse.psd file, 128
    Oil Medium Brush Wet Edges, 129
    printing, 143
    Watercolor filter, 128
    Wet Media brushes, 129

watercolor example II
    Cookie Cutter tool, 143
    fills, 143
    Flatten image, 141
    Levels adjustment, 141
    masks, 143
    Texturizer, 143
Watercolor filter
    pop art example, 15
    watercolor example, 128
Wave filter, currency example, 25
Weathered copper text, horizontal Type tool, 226
weathered copper text
    Bevels layer, 226
    Horizontal Type tool, 226
    Hue/Saturation, 227
    Shape tool, 227
    stoned.psd file, 226
Wet Media brushes, watercolor example, 129

windmills example
    Blend mode, 116
    drop shadows, 119
    Gradient Mills dialog box, 117
    gradients, 117
    layers, 116
    Styles and Effects palette, 119
    Type tool, 118
    warped text, 118
    Windmill.psd file, 116
Windows clipboard, copy to, 9
WOW-Chrome Reflecting layer style
    oriental display box, 173
    power type, 221
WOW-Plastic Clear layer style, twisted steel example, 171

X-Y-Z

young woman in shadows.psd, master image and, 133
Young woman standing.psd file, size relationships and, 165
zoom, frames example, 74